Who's Your FRIEND?

ATO BAILEY

Co/Author Pastor Peacelyn Blankson

MINISTRYHOUSE
publications
www.ministryhouse.com

Who is Your Friend

Author: Ato Bailey
Co/Author: Pastor Peacelyn Blankson
Copyright © Ato Bailey 2013

Author:	Ato Bailey
Email:	atobailey@yahoo.com
	nobleschapel@yahoo.com

Contact: Pastor Peacelyn Blankson
Los Angeles, CA(USA)
323-617-7199

ISBN-13: 978-1516806249
ISBN-10: 1516806247

Words meaning are taken from the King Version Bible

All rights reserved. No part of this book may be reproduced or transmitted in any form or by any means, electronic or mechanical including photocopying, recording or otherwise by any information storage and retrieval system, without prior permission in writing from the publisher.

INDEX

Dedication	6
Note of thanks	7
Foreword	8
chapter 1 The nature of friendship	11
chapter 2 The importance of friendship	17
chapter 3 The joy of friendship	49
chapter 4 What does the bible say? about friendship?	57
chapter 5 Friendship and respect	79
chapter 6 Types of friendship	87
chapter 7 When friendship hurts	149
chapter 8 Friendship and argument	193
chapter 9 Overcoming rejection	203
chapter 10 Friendship with the wealthy	225
chapter 11 Friendship and gifts	237
chapter 12 Jesus, friend of all	255

Dedication

This book is dedicated to the LORD JESUS CHRIST
&
My lovely daughter: Ewurafua Bailey

Note of Thanks

Many thanks to the following people for the love and support given to me:
My elder brother, Mr. Edwin Kofi Mould- Bailey,
Pastor Kofi Livingstone of Resurrection Power Ministries Amsterdam and
John & Shakila Olsen of Galilee Publication. Thanks to my sister Stella Bailey, who has been an encourager and to all Bailey family

Foreword

In my own experience of life, it has become obviously clear and apparent to me, in the times we live, the true meaning of friendship and love have been greatly diluted, misused, misunderstood and misinterpreted. Therefore, my motivation to research, explore and write this book, were to position the origins and biblical understanding and make an attempt to share the truth for clear understanding.

Firstly, let us look at the words origins according to noted dictionaries and the bible:

According to the Oxford Dictionary: (UK)
Origin: Old English 'frēondscipe' (see friend, -ship). Friend means: a person with whom one has a bond of mutual affection, typically one exclusive of sexual, personal or family relations. Friendship is simply, the emotions or conduct of friends; the state of being friends.

Noah Webster Dictionary: (America's 1st dictionary)
In the nineteenth century defined a person experiencing the trappings of this word as, one who is attached to another by love; One who entertains for another's sentiment of esteem, respect and affection, which leads him to desire his company and to seek to promote his happiness and prosperity.

Friend or Friendship: What is the origin and how has the meaning changed over time? The words friend and friendship are out of the many words whose meaning have remained consistent in the English language. The word Friend emanated from the word 'Freond' from the verb, 'Freon', which means; to love or to be mutually affectionate.

With the passage of time the meaning of these words have remained, but have been developed to include all the essential ingredients needed to make their meaning clear. We can conclude, then, these words are basically grounded on LOVE, without which, are impossible to define. In other words, we can confidently say, that a friend is one who is interested in doing something for another person because it is an essential part of the former.

Jesus demonstrated the importance of friendship and love to the human race by laying down His glorious life in heaven to buy man's salvation with His blood. He did it freely, so that anybody who enjoys his friendship would also share in His kingdom. This is what a friend does. A friend often sticks closer than even blood relations.

We may have many acquaintances we sometimes mistake to be friends, but true friendship is more scarce. Friendship goes beyond the normal greeting, but in a personal relationship that is grounded in a concern for each other's welfare; this involves a degree of intimacy.

According to the bible we look at; King Solomon's 'Song of Songs,' which was originally written in the Hebrew language, having at least 3 different words for our English word 'Love.'

The first word we find is the word 'raya'. Raya would be translated, literally, as friend, or companion, 'somebody to hang out with and/or soul mate.'

The second Hebrew word we find for love is 'ahava.'
Ahava is the love of the will. Now, this is way more profound than fleeting romantic feelings. This is much more than

temporary urges. Ahava is making a decision to join your life to the life of another. This is the emotion that leads to committed relationship.

The third Hebrew word for love that we find in the Song of Songs is the word 'dod'.
Dod is translated in English, literally as to 'carouse' to 'rock' or to 'fondle.' Dod is the phyisical, sexual element to a relationship.

As author and theologian Rob Bell quoted;
"We have our raya flame. We have our ahava flame. And, we have our dod flame.
One flame burning all on its own will never be as hot as all these flames burning together.
I mean, we were created for all the flames to burn as one."

I invite you to read on to discover the many elements and perceptions of friendship, In the hope you gain an insight to reaffirm the true meaning and apply it to your life.

"I PRAY THIS BOOK WILL ENABLE YOU TO DETERMINE THE TRUE UNDERSTANDING OF FRIENDSHIP; AND ENCOURAGE YOU TO SEARCH YOURSELF AND SEE WHERE YOU FALL SHORT TO HAVING OR BEING A FRIEND. THE CHAPTERS THAT FOLLOW DELVE INTO THE SUBJECT MATTER WITH THE AIM OF SIMPLIFYING AND AROUSING YOUR INTEREST TO APPRECIATE THE TRUE MEANING"

chapter 1

THE NATURE OF FRIENDSHIP

"Greater love has no man than this that a man (a friend) lay down his life for his friends" (John 15: 13)

Life is the most valuable thing a person can ever posses, because without it one's existence ceases. Thus, laying down one's life for the sake of a friend shows the extent of one's love. This is precisely what Jesus Christ left His heavenly throne and glory to do for mankind. It is not surprising that He asks His followers to 'endeavour' to be like him. Friendship basically requires a distinctive kind of concern for each other.

Three words in the Ancient Greek language give a vivid and excellent explanation of the word, they are; **Eros, Agape and Philia.**

Eros; or 'erotic love' expresses sexual love or the feelings of arousal shared by two persons who are physically attracted to one another.

Agape; 'love is love', which is of and from God, whose very nature is selfless love. The Apostle John asserts this in

1 John 4:8 "God is love." God does not merely love; He is love itself. Everything God does flows from this love. It is vital to note that God's love is not a 'selfish,' sentimental love such as portrayed by many people. God loves because that is the expression of His being. He loves the unlovable not because we deserve to be loved, but because He must be true to His personality and character. This is the love Christ portrayed on the Cross of Calvary. In the same way, we are to love others sacrificially. Jesus gave the parable of the Good Samaritan as an example of sacrifice for the sake of others, even for those who may not care about, or even hate us, as the Jews did the Samaritans. Sacrificial love is not based on feelings; it is a determined act of the will, a blissful steadfastness to put the well-being of others above our own. This type of love does not come naturally to humans.

Philia is the ancient Greek word for 'neighbourly love', the bonds of friendship that bind us together in a community. It originally meant a kind of affectionate regard or friendly feeling not just for one's friends, but also towards family members, relatives, church members, business partners and one's country and community at large. This is the kind of love Jesus talked about when He commanded that we love our neighbours as ourselves. *(See: Matthew 19: 19)*

Given these classifications of the word love, ***philia*** seems to be one most pertinent to friendship. For this reason, love and friendship are used interchangeably as a single topic. In spite of closeness in meaning, there are significant differences between them. Love is an attitude directed at a particular person, whether or not there is an established relationship with that person. Friendship, on the other hand, is a relationship grounded in a special concern one has for the other.

A PREPARED FRIEND: What are gifts meant for, if not to comfort and beautify us? Friends can be a form of talents or gifts God has endowed us with, just as a tree is God's gift of shelter or food etc. Our friends are blessed with different talents that we need to help us develop our own talents, and to endure the pressures of this world. Our friends also serve different purposes because there is a time for every purpose and work. For example, the Bible recounts that God prepared a tree to cover Jonah and to serve as a shade (shadow) over his head to bring him relief in his grief. *(See: Jonah 4: 6)* Jesus Christ also announced Himself as living water, which His followers need to quench their thirst *(See: John 4: 14)*. This is what friends should exist for: to be always there for one another; to clothe one another and lend a helping hand when needed. With this understanding I can confidently refer to a friend as a well and spring meant to quench the other's thirst. Friends help in times when things are beyond the other's reach. God has made provisions for all that His children need each moment of our lives. He is available to us to the extent we also make ourselves available to Him, and much the same way we avail ourselves to our friends and they to us. As 'Teofil Paraianu' observes, "Take my friends away, pour my friends out of me, empty me of them and you will find that nothing would remain of me."

AFFINITY: 'The *Macmillan Essential Dictionary*,' defines affinity as a feeling that you understand and like someone or something because they are like you. With this definition, I ask the question: what does it take to maintain and grow a friendship? Friendship involves connection at a deeper and personal level. It involves empathy, sympathy, likeness, fellow-feeling, among others things. It is not necessarily an expression of emotions, but getting excited over the fact that you have found someone you can share and ponder over things with. Emotions become involved when you meet someone you agree with and this is what arouses emotions at those times. You are blessed if you find a good friend with whom you have a deep agreement. A friend is not literally another self, but one who shares many of your interests, values, ideas, and perspectives. If a friend were truly another self, then I would need but one friend; and it is because a friend is not quite another self, but sees life from different stance than you do, therefore, you need multiple friends with whom you can explore different positive aspects of life. Renowned Canadian Psychotherapist, Nathaniel Branden noted; *"a friend is a mirror who reflects my soul back to me."*

FRIENDS ARE NOT ACCIDENTS: The popular saying of believers that *'nothing happens to God's children by accident' is perfectly true'*. Friends in your present life are not there by accident but because the Lord allowed them to come into contact with you. There is no human friendship which is void of problems (moral): misunderstandings or hurts etc. Professor of Philosophy, James Grunebaun asserts that; "it is sometimes morally justifiable to prefer one's friends to non-friends. He tackles the familiar tussle between feelings; that friends deserve special attention, and demands justly that we treat all persons equally."He continues; "the answer to this conflict depends on the answer to the more basic question, what is friendship?"For Aristotle (ancient Greek philosopher), "friendship is an integral part of life worth living and each friend fits into a hierarchy of more or less perfect forms of human activity."The relationship between husband and wife, father and son, neighbours, business partners, team members, members of a political party, teacher and student, and so on, would all be viewed as friendship in Aristotle's eye.

'A friend in need is a friend indeed', and such friends, I say again, are not easy to come by. When you have found such a man or woman, and tested the sincerity of their friendship; hold on to him or her with strong hands and never let them go. It may be that because they are a faithful friend but will sometimes make you angry. See how Solomon put it: "Open rebuke is better than secret love. Faithful are the wounds of a friend." *(Proverbs 27: 5 - 6)*

It takes a great deal of closeness to be able to tell the mistakes or faults of a person to their face. Friends do not flatter; true friends speak at the right time and, if need be, even speak so sharply as to cause a scare (open rebuke). If you are unworthy of your friend, you will begin to get tired of them when they decide to perform on your behalf the true act of charity by warning you of a danger, and reminding you of your shortcomings.

BIBLICAL EXAMPLES OF FRIENDSHIP: King Solomon, knowing one of the greatest tests of friendship among imperfect beings like us, reiterates the importance of a true friend: *"Your own friend and your fathers Friend forsake not." (Proverbs 27: 10)*.

Many stories are recounted in the Bible, both from the Old and New Testaments about the value of friendship; true friendship is a treasure to unearth. Abraham is referred to as a 'Friend of God', because of his intimate relationship with God. God spoke to Moses face to face as a man unto his friend; the 'romantic' friendship of Ruth and Naomi, the devotion of the subordinate Hushai to David, or the mutual relation between David and Jonathan are all worthy of emulation.

In the storehouse of private thought, you find a large area reserved for this question: ***Who is my friend?*** Such a question arises when life becomes too burdensome to be lived constantly alone. Who do I really know? What man or woman in my world would take the time to hear me out if I had talk about some heavy stuff? Who will come running to my side when I am in real trouble? Is there any man or woman who sees me as having something to offer or give? When was the last time I conversed and chatted with someone I call a friend? How did I ever get so lonely? Apparently, thoughts like these run through the minds of all men and women. However, what I have come to understand is that friendship does not just happen; it is sought after, developed, and maintained. Friendships are not accidental or self- perpetuating. They must be cultivated much as a shrub is carefully planted and tended into a tree. What many people fail to understand is; there is much that one can do to maintain the people around one self, rather than the deception that causes many people to stay away from each other. The fact is, every human being needs friendship with other human beings.

chapter 2

THE IMPORTANCE OF FRIENDSHIP

"And the next day we landed at Sidon; and Julius, in kindness to Paul, allowed him to go to his friends so they might provide for his needs." (Acts 27: 3)

And when he finds it, he joyfully puts it on his shoulder and goes home. Then he calls his friends and neighbours together and says, rejoice with me; I have found my lost sheep. (Luke 15: 6)

Julius the centurion was an extraordinary civilian to Paul. Paul was committed to him as a prisoner; he treated him as a man that had an interest in heaven and a friend. It is a beautiful principle of our nature, that deep feelings, either sorrow or joy, are almost too much for one to bear alone, and that there is a feeling of positive relief in having friends to share with. The causes of modern social problems ranging from divorce to homelessness or obesity to addiction are often thought to be associated to poverty, stress or unhappiness. But the word of God notes emphatically that we are overlooking something crucial: *friendship.* It appears that our society is ignoring its importance. The Greek philosopher Aristotle said;

"In poverty and other misfortunes of life, true friends are a sure refuge. They keep the young out of wicked deeds; they comfort and aid the old in their weakness, and they incite those in the prime of life to noble deeds."

Friendship is vital to the well-being of mankind, but takes a great deal of time to develop. Friendship is not an inborn thing which comes to a person by virtue of the fact that he or she is in this world; anyone with this kind of reasoning stands the risk of being neglected. Friendship is most valued, especially during difficult times. If you asked most people why they became homeless, why their marriage failed or why they over ate, they would often respond that it was because of the poor quality, or non-existence of friendship; the absence of love.

RESEARCH OF TOM RATH: Tom Rath undertook a study of friendship, alongside several leading researchers. His work resulted in some surprising statistics: if your best friend eats healthily, you are five times more likely to have a healthy diet yourself. Married people say that friendship is five times more important than physical intimacy within marriage. Those who say they have no real friends at work have only one in twelve chances of feeling engaged in their job.

Time magazine once noted; *"Let friendship ring. It might look like idle chatter, but when employees find friends at work, they feel connected to their jobs. Having a best friend at work is a strong predictor for being a happy and productive employee."*

RECOGNITION OF FRIENDSHIP: To recognize which of your friendships provides you with the different things you need, sharpen its strength. Of course, it is not always a good idea to judge friends in a detached way, or to doubt a friendship just because you cannot easily identify its rewards. The closest friends like each other for who they are in themselves, not for what they deliver! The Lord Jesus Christ made the point that it is better to give than to receive. Aristotle said; friendship comes with living what he called a good life, including strong personal values such as honesty, character and passion. The British writer, Mark Vernon, wrote: *"The noble man is most involved with wisdom and friendship."* Oscar Wilde also emphasized the devoted aspect of true friendship when he said, *"Anybody can sympathise with the suffering of a friend, but it requires a very fine nature to appreciate a friend's success."* Ralph Emerson said, *"A friend is a person with whom I may be sincere."*

The word of God recounts that money does not buy happiness. Aristotle suggested that we spend at least a fifth of our time with our friends. He asked; is this not what children do in their persistent request to play with their friends? A close friend is a mirror of your own self, someone with whom you realize that, though autonomous, you are not alone. Friendship is also in politics because it "grows the virtues, such as creativity and compassion, which are essential to a flourishing society." if we cultivate friendship, we can lift some of the burden from our apparently unhappy, isolated lives, homes, societies and nations.

EXPECTATIONS IN FRIENDSHIP:

"Do not hold back good from those who deserve it, when it is in the power of your hand. Do not say to your neighbor or friend, "come back later; I will give it tomorrow" when you now have it with you." (Proverbs 3: 27)

We have a reference to duty in a moral sense. We have the duty of friendship, that which is due to friends. The ancient Greek word for duty, **opheilo**, means to *'to owe'*, *'to be due'*. It also means an obligatory task or service rendered to God and man (I.e. friends). The Lord Jesus Christ sums up man's duty in His commandment to "Love God and love your neighbor (friend) as yourself. Every person owes his friend a duty. Duties vary according to one's relationship with another. Thus, every person has a duty to God, self, family, state and friends.

"Eat, O friends, and drink; drink your fill, O lover."
(King Solomon's Songs of Songs 5: 1)

"The next day we landed at Sidon; and Julius, in kindness to Paul, allowed him to go to his friends so they might provide for his needs." (Acts 27: 3)

God, here encourages those that suffer for Him to trust in Him; for He puts into their hearts those to befriend, for who they least expect can cause them to be pitied. God causes His beloved to be prized and valued, even in the eyes of their enemies. This is probably the reason why Paul's friends took it upon themselves to make his situation and journey as comfortable as possible.

HOSPITALITY: A friend should readily and cheerfully entertain his friend(s). This is a duty which is frequently exhibited by a true friend. They should be hospitable one to another without a grudge. By caring and entertaining friends you may, perhaps, be honored with the presence of people whose company could bring you honor and blessings. We would do well not to miss the privilege of relating closely with a good friend in a mutual conversation and prayer. The blessings such a friend could bring will worth far more than it will cost us to entertain him or her. Never miss the opportunity to extend hospitality to a friend, for, by so doing, you may unknowingly be entertaining angels.

Abraham extended hospitality to an angel of the Lord. Though you may not have a similar experience, what you do to friends, in obedience to Him (God), is seen and accepted by Him and will not go unrewarded *(Matt 25: 31-40)*. God has often poured honor and favor on dutiful and hospitable friends beyond their imagination. A friend should show works of charity to others by providing food for the hungry and clothes for the naked. God has deposited in you the power to do good to your needy friends; you should not neglect them. It is the lack of faith which generally produces hard-heartedness towards your friends.

Some friends pretend not to see or know those troubled, because they have no desire to help their friends; but ignorance will not profit them. A true friend will not frustrate the desire and hope of his friend, or disappoint a friend in need when he has the capacity to offer the expected assistance. He should share his blessings with the needy, no matter how little they may be.

Sharing is in line with the law of hospitality. It is a law among the *'Arabian people'* that a friend shall always be helped first, and offered that which is best, no matter how needy the friend may be. Their settled laws of hospitality demand that the friend receive the first and the best portion. This law of duty and hospitality, Job said, he has carefully observed, and has not held back what he has received from his friends, the poor and fatherless:

"If I have denied the distress of the poor or let the eyes of the widow grow weary, if I have kept my bread to myself, not sharing it with the fatherless, but from my youth I reared him as would a father, and from my birth I guided the widow. If I have seen anyone perishing for lack of clothing or a needy man without a garment, the man who was dying I blessed; I made the widow's heart sing. I was eyes to the blind and feet to the lame. I rescued the poor who cried for help and the fatherless who had none to assist him. I was a father to the needy; I took up the case of the stranger. I broke the jaw of the wicked and snatched the victims from their teeth." (Job 29: 11-17).

Job's friends and associates testified about him like a magistrate or judge, he was a patron to his friends. A true friend should desire Job's spirit. The duty of a true friend is to become a patron; by vindicating his or her friend(s), and saving him or her from any form of oppression. He should be his or her counselor, guide, assistant and benefactor. He should take him or her under his protection, and treat him or her as he would his own child. *"A man, who claims the office of a good friend, should love everything about his friend, and be ready to promote him to great honor".* A dutiful friend becomes all things to his friends, and wins their heart. A friend who neglects his or her duty to the poor, but is frequent in his or her visit or duty to the rich, knows little about true friendship, and has little of God's Spirit indwelling in him or her. How unfit are the self-opinionated, the self -loving, self-seeking, self-confident and self-pleasing, having little regard or respect for others, being proud, stubborn, forward, and inflexible, making themselves the attraction to be called dutiful friends! The friend who loves his or her friend gives himself or herself totally to help him or her. Such friends are those God promotes, favors and exalts. How dutiful are you to your friend? Who is your friend?

Here are some duties of true friendship: True hearts give rise to certain duties to friendship. True hands confer (to grant as a gift or benefit) on their friends certain rights concerning their property, persons, tongue and heart by way of forgiveness, sincerity, loyalty, relief and consideration. This comprises seven duties in all:

FIRST DUTY:

Daeron of House Gwydion said: *"Two friends are likened to a pair of hands, one of which washes the other."* He chooses the simile of the two hands, rather than the feet, because the pair offers mutual assistance towards a single aim. So it is with two friends; their friendship is only complete when they are comrades in a single enterprise. In a sense, the two are like one person. Their friendship entails a common participation in good fortune and bad, a partnership in the future as in the present moment, an abandonment of possessiveness and selfishness. There are thus three degrees in sharing one's property with one's friend:

- The lowest degree is when you place your friend on the same footing as your slave or servant, and attend to his or her need from your surplus.

- At the second degree you place your friend on the same footing as yourself. You are content to have him or her as a partner in your property and to treat him or her the way you would treat yourself.

- At the third degree, the highest of all, you prefer your friend to yourself and set his or her need before your own.

SECOUND DUTY:

"Do not withhold good from those who deserve it, when it is in your power to act. Do not say to your neighbor, 'Come back later; I will give it tomorrow' when you now have it with you." (Proverbs 3: 27-28)

The second duty is to render personal aid in the satisfaction of needs, attending to your friends without waiting to be asked, and giving them priority over private needs. The first illustration of the duty of friendly love is readiness to serve. He who is in need has a claim of ownership upon our property by the law of love, which is the law of God. The good, which you can and ought to give, is not yours but the property of your needy friend. Needs make the poor (friend) owner, and God makes you the supplier of the goods which you have, and which the poor needs. We must refuse nothing good (nothing either legally or morally good) to him who has a right to it. A true friend should not make excuses to shift a duty that must be done immediately, or delight in keeping a friend in suspense, or show the authority the giver has over the needy. A true friend acts readily and cheerfully, and from a principle of a clear conscience towards God. If your friend has a need, and you have the ability to supply it, you must look upon it as his or her and not hold it back. Do not refuse kindness to your friend when it is in your power to perform it.

Here are three degrees as in the case of material support: the lowest degree involves attending to the need, when asked and when in abundance, with joy and cheerfulness, showing pleasure and gratitude. Your friend's need should be seen as your need, or even more important than your need. You should look out for times of need, and not wait to be begged to do what you should consider a duty for which you receive God's blessing. And in meeting such needs, your generosity should be limitless.

THIRD DUTY:

"Make it your ambition to lead a quiet life, to mind your own business and to work with your hands, just as we told you." (1 Thessalonians 4: 11)

The third duty concerns the tongue, which should know when to speak out or be silent. Here is an exhortation to orderly and peaceful living among friends. No friend should be engaged in foolish talk or identify with any form of excitement, which is capable of leading to disorder and disregard of friendship. Gracious speech is to be regarded as a sacred duty. Make it your aim to be quiet. It is a most desirable thing to have a calm and quiet temper, and to exhibit a peaceful and quiet behavior. This will enhance your own happiness and that of others (friends) around you. Friends should study when to speak and when to be quiet. A true friend should be ambitious and industrious, calm and patient and exhibit a harmonious disposition, not giving in to gossip and destructive criticism that leads to division. Satan's eternal strategy is to make you talkative, which you have the tendency to be as a human being. This is the more reason why you should learn to be quiet and not to talk unnecessarily.

DO NOT CONTRADICT HIM OR HER: Do not mention a friend's faults in his or her presence or absence. Do not openly contradict, dispute or argue with him or her. Do not secretly pry into his or her affairs. Keep his or her secrets confided in you and on no account disclose them to a third party; not even to their closest friends. Do not reveal anything about them, not even after separation and conflict, for to do so would amount to 'meanness' on your part. Avoid criticizing his or her dear ones; also from relating other people's criticism of him or her, for it is your informant who directly abuses you. Of course you should not hide any praise you may hear, for the pleasure in it, is received directly from the conveyor of the compliment, as well as indirectly from the original source. If you keep such compliments to yourself it smacks of envy. In short, you should avoid relating unpleasant speech in general, unless you are obliged to speak out to promote good and prevent evil, and even then, only if you can find no valid excuse for saying nothing. In such cases you need not worry about your friend's disapproval, since your action would be beneficial to them when rightly understood, even if it initially looks bad.

HOLD YOUR TONGUE: Just as it is proper for you to hold your tongue from openly mentioning a friend's faults, so ought you to observe silence in your heart. This is done by giving up suspicions, for suspicions breed bitterness, which is also unlawful. Keep within the bounds by not misinterpreting his or her actions, so long as you accept them in good faith. As for what is unintentionally revealed, and over you had no control, you should, if possible, ascribe what you witness to absent-mindedness and forgetfulness.

Part of this matter is to keep quiet, and not disclose a friend's secret entrusted to you. Silence includes staying away from contention and contradicting whatever your friend says. While it is his or her decision to reveal the secret to whoever he or she wishes to know it, you would maintain a clear conscience by dutifully keeping quiet. For to remain silent when one is right is harder on the soul than keeping quiet when one is wrong. The most serious issues that instigate hatred between friends are arguments and quarrels. They are the very source of differences and rupture (breaking apart), for separation begins with differences in opinions, and then escalates into verbal attacks and, finally, physical confrontation(s). The worst disgrace is contention, for if you reject outright what another says, you accuse him or her of ignorance and stupidity, or of forgetfulness and absent-mindedness in a given subject or matter. All this leads to disgrace, annoyance and unfriendliness. In general, the only motive for this struggle among friends is to display intellectual superiority and belittle one's opponent by exposing his or her ignorance. This leads to arrogance, bitterness, hurt and insults. If there is no other reason for hatred and avoidance but this, why should it be permitted to intrude into true friendship?

THE FOURTH DUTY:

"And sound speech that cannot be condemned, so that those who oppose you may be ashamed because they have nothing bad to say about us. (Titus 2: 8)

"Let your conversation be always full of grace, seasoned with salt, so that you may know to answer everyone." (Colossians 4: 6)

"Do not let any unwholesome talk come out of your mouths, but let what is helpful for building others up according their needs, that it may benefit those who listen." (Ephesians 4: 29)

A true friend uses language that promotes peace and cordiality. Your words should not be weak or unsound; words no one could find fault with. You should use words that really portrays your godly nature; the Christ in you. You should be courteous and agreeable. Let the words that proceed out of your mouth be fresh, full of wisdom, excluding all "corrupt communication." Harsh would only repel those you relate with friends.

"He who talks for the mere sake of talking will say many foolish things; He whose great aim in life is to benefit others, will not be likely to say that which he have occasion to **regret."**

It is a great duty for friends to carefully choose their words in order not to offend with their lips, and that they improve words and speech, as much as possible, for the good of others. A friend should be bold to speak; cowards are not true friends. True friends see the worst of their friends, and are not afraid to advise them. Their confidence gives them courage, and the courage protects them from the power of fear and silence.

EXPRESSION OF AFFECTION: The fourth duty is to use the tongue to speak out positively or negatively without stepping on the toes of a friend. Just as friendship calls for silence about unpleasant things, it also requires the utterance of favorable things. The best way to avoid hurting your friends is not to hurt them; that is to say that, 'you do unto them as you want them to do unto you'. You should indicate by word and deed, when you disapprove of any circumstance that is disagreeable, also let them know in plain language that you share their joy in all situations that give them pleasure as well; friendship means participating together in joy and in sadness.

You must communicate to them the praise of anyone who praises them; showing your pleasure, for to hide such praise would be pure envy. Furthermore, you should thank him or her for what he or she does for, or on your behalf. What is more honorable is defending them in their absence whenever they are abused or their honour is attacked. Friendship calls for protection, rebuke and defence whenever the need arises.

THE FIFTH DUTY:

"For if you forgive men when they sin against you, your heavenly Father will also forgive you; But if you do not forgive men their sins, your Father will not forgive your sins." (Matthew 6: 14-15)

Be kind and compassionate to one another, forgiving each other, just as in Christ forgave you. (Ephesians 4: 32)

Forgiveness is emphasized regularly in the Bible. Our Savior reiterates that we forgive even when the same offence is repeated seventy times seven times. By this He means that when a man or neighbor or friend asks for forgiveness, we are to constantly pardon the offence since it is impossible to count the same offence seventy times seven times. How absurd such counting would be! We are to declare our willingness to forgive without measure. If the offender does not even ask for our forgiveness, we are to forgive the fellow in our hearts and deeds. Never harbor malice, nor speak ill of a person you call and accept as a friend. One of the most difficult things human beings are called to do by God is to respond to evil with kindness and to forgive what appears to be the unforgivable. To forgive the failings of your friends is the best thing you can do for yourself. Your friend may not deserve to be forgiven for the pain and suffering purposefully inflicted on your life, but you deserve to be free of this canker of unforgiveness.

SET A PRISONER FREE:

'To forgive is to set a prisoner free and discover the prisoner was you'

'Two persons cannot be friends if they cannot forgive each other's little failings.'

Your refusal to forgive the mistakes of a friend eventually leads to entrapment, estrangement and resentment.

Entrapment is much like attaching yourself to an anchor and dropping it into the sea.

Estrangement is to make someone (you used to show affection to) hostile or to remove or dissociate oneself from society (friendship). That is to say that you want those (friends) who hurt you to suffer as you have.

Resentment is anger and ill-will with respect to real or fancied wrong or injury. It also means to feel something again. That is when you rehearse the offence over and over again. You must learn or strive to let go of wrongs done to you by friends so that you can experience the freedom, joy and beauty of friendship.

Having a very good friend hurt you, is one of the worst feelings you can possibly imagine. The pain can be overwhelming. You feel as if a knife has cut through your back and will never heal. Friendship that is marked by knowledge, trust and appreciation, can stand the test of time: quarrels, disagreements, etc. Such friendship is easy to rebuild when there is a crack somewhere. You can start all over with your friend only after you have learnt to forgive his or her mistake(s) . You can forgive, but forgetting is not easy. They must earn your trust again.

"A friend should be able to have pity, compassion and to show kindness in spite of the faults of his or her erring friend; for so is true friendship." I ask you again, 'Who is your friend?'

THE SIXTH DUTY:

Loyalty and Sincerity: "To him that is afflicted pity should be shown from his friend." (Job 6: 14)

"A friend loves at all times, and a brother is born for adversity." (Proverbs 17: 17)

"And his friends heard of it, they went out lay hold on him: for they said He is beside himself." (Mark 3: 21)

"Therefore dear friends, since you already know this, are on your guard so that you may not be carried away by the error of lawless men and fall from your steadfastness." (Loyalty and Sincerity). (2 Peter 3: 17)

The *Oxford Advanced Learner's Dictionary (UK)* defines loyalty as the quality of being faithful in your support of something or somebody. By this definition I can firmly assert that one of the most desirable qualities to be found in any individual should be loyalty. Loyalty is the faithful, consistent exercise of and devotion to a duty or obligation owed someone or something. It implies unswerving allegiance to something or someone. Our first loyalty should be to God and then mankind. This is borne out in the words of Jesus when He says; "Thou shall love the Lord thy God with all thy heart, and with all thy soul, and with thy entire mind". The second is: "thou shall love thy neighbour as thyself." *(Matthew 22: 37-39)*

True friendship is built upon loyalty, faith, sincerity and co-operation. You must be fully convinced in your heart about anything and everything you get involved in. To be a loyal and sincere friend requires what I call 'full persuasion'. This is to say that if you are not persuaded in whatever you stand for, there is no way you can defend or love the thing. It is the same with friendship; you must be persuaded so that nothing destroys your relationship. If you are going to be loyal and sincere to your friend, you will have to be loyal and sincere to yourself first. A loyal and sincere friend is open and shares happiness, sorrow and joy with you. Everything has a price: marriage, education, raising children, and so on.

Loyalty is what makes a man stay glued to his wife for many years without committing adultery; loyalty is what makes a parent dedicate his life savings to the education of his children without any regrets, and so on. It was Jonathan's loyalty to David, which saved the life of David from the hands of Saul. To be loyal to someone means you cannot be loyal to everyone; you will love one and hate the other. Friendships cannot and should not be taken for granted. They are not meaningless; they should mean something to us. The friends you choose must contribute something positively in your life and vice versa. I would advise all friends to protect and maintain their friendships by being loyal and sincere.

CONSIDER ALL: The meaning of loyalty is steadfastness in love and maintaining it in all conditions and circumstances with your friend(s). If it is severed before death the work is in vain and the effort wasted. Loyalty to a friend includes of all he or she holds sacred: wife, husband, children, parent, siblings and dependants. Consideration is a great duty among friends. Nothing proves the strength of compassion and love so much, as when these are carried over from a loved one to his or her siblings, parents or dependants. True friends must show concern; that is, care for each other no matter what the other's situation is. Let not friends forget themselves, who are in the state of destroying themselves by debaucheries. There is shame on people who choose to despise their friends. If there is any occasion when kindness, loyalty and sincerity should be shown, it is when your friend is sinking in sorrow and pain. He or she, who forsakes the fear of God, fails to console his or her friend. It is not true friendship, if it is not constant, loyal and sincere. Those friends that are fanciful or selfish in their friendship will love no longer than their humor is pleased and their best interest served, therefore, their affection turns with the wind and changes with the weather. To be loyal and sincere to your friend means being careful and appreciating their pain. A true friend is born to support and comfort others in distress. Your loyalty to your friend(s) is very important. An unstable friend is no friend at all. To be loyal and sincere in a friendship, demands self-denial, love, discipline and prayer. Who then is your friend?

HOW TO MAKE FRIENDS: There is a form of beauty in being alone. You have more time to do the things you want to do, like introspective walks, reading books and other private endeavors. If you want to share your options, though, there are billions of potential friends in the world. Many of these want to make friends just as much as you do. So consider these suggestions to meet people for strong, lasting friendships.

A man who has friends must show himself to be friendly (i.e. social). He who is friendly will have friends. If you wish to be loved, show yourself as loving. Having too many friends can lead to our downfall. It is not the multitude of friends that help us. What we should value is the one whose love is stronger and purer even than all ties of siblings. He who is friendly will have friends. There are friends who can help to bring you down; or a man or woman of many friends comes to a loss, is defeated and fails. A person without a definite and decisive character cannot make lasting friends. The true friend is the one who remains true in good, difficult and odd times. To have friends and keep them, we must not quarrel with them, but must love them by being free with them, pleasing them, visiting them, and especially, serving them in everything that lies within our power; that is showing ourselves to be friendly.

In summary, 'to make friends, show yourself to be friendly'.

SPEND TIME AROUND PEOPLE:

'Those that would make friends must spend time around people and in their case, they must be where they are, put themselves in their condition and speak kindly and familiarly to them of the things of God and the affairs of life.' (Refer: Ezekiel 3: 14-15 & Matthew 11: 19).

Friends seldom come knocking on your door while you are home. If the people you are already around (e.g. at work, school, etc.) are not good material to be friends, for whatever reasons, it's not the end of the world. You do not necessarily have to have a lot in common interest with people in order to make friends with them. Some of the most rewarding friendships are between two people who do not have much in common at all. However, when you have something in common with people, it can make it easier to make friends. No one would get very much out of life if he or she lived absolutely alone. It is the strong connection, sweet satisfying communion with other people that makes life worth living. One reason why, so many people are disappointed with what life has in store for them, is because they have never improved upon their ability to make and keep friends. Many people have been great social mixers, but only outwardly.

Inwardly, they feel very lonely and isolated. They have wrapped themselves in their own selfishness, viewing all others simply in relation to their own self-gratification. To live so, whatever our social status may be, sooner or later brings an ironic sense of having had no real joy at all, and makes the late Lord Beaconsfield's famous words seem so true; *"Youth is a mistake, manhood a struggle, and old age regret."* What a different view of life we get when we see it through the eyes of the Lord Jesus. With Jesus there is no viewing of life selfishly rather than socially. None was ever so social-minded as He. He went around doing only good. He was the best of all mixers and was at home in every circle, for wherever He was, He was there to forget Himself for the good of others. And with Him there was no viewing of the human life as apart from God. He was God's hand in everything and everywhere. Life is not a mockery. God is love, and He wants us to love all men, in spite of their condition in life. Behind every frowning circumstance is a smiling face. Don't give pity, give action and bless somebody with a smile. Make friends and be a real friend to someone today!

TALK TO PEOPLE: Each time you talk to somebody you have the chance of making a lasting friend. You do not have to be in an organization to talk to people. You can talk to anybody at any given time; the person sitting next to you in the conference or seminar, on the bus, the person in front of you in the dinner queue, in church and so on.

There are many ways to do this, for example: a comment about your immediate environment, request for help, giving a compliment so many ways! Keep the conversation light on at all times and be cheery. When you are complaining about something, make sure it is something you are both dissatisfied with. Introduce yourself towards the end of the conversation. It can be as simple as saying: "Oh, by the way, my name is……" once you have introduced yourself, the other person will do likewise. Remember his or her name; it is important.

Openness means being ready and free for engagement. It is to be more receptive to new ideas or other opinions. You can talk your heart out, but it will not gain you a friend if you do not open up into a real conversation. Remember, you have 2 ears and one mouth, so listen twice as long as you talk. When you have had your heart broken in a relationship, it can be difficult to open up to love again and commend your heart to another person. Similarly, when your friend hurts you, it can be difficult to open up and bring back the trust into your friendship. It is hard to give your heart back to someone who has proven hurtful.

ASSUME THEY LIKE YOU: Assume that any person close to you will eventually hurt you, and continue to hurt you periodically. Have you ever hurt the people you love? Was it intentional, malicious? Were you sorry afterwards? Did you have trouble admitting remorse? When others hurt you, realize they are just like you. They have very likely hurt you unintentionally, and are genuinely sorry afterwards. Don't do anything to pressure someone into being a friend. Do try to change yourself in order to fit in to enhance making new friends. Never blame the "friend-to-be" for failing to invite you to a church, crusade, party, etc; don't call "the friend-to-be" repeatedly or stop by uninvited, unless you have established that stopping-by-unannounced practice is agreeable; and refrain from overstaying your welcome anywhere. In general take friendship slowly, and don't try to force intimacy to grow quickly. Once you have started the friendship, remember to do your part by initiating some of the activities, remembering birthdays, asking how the other person is feeling, or else the friendship will become unbalanced and an uneasiness and distance is likely to arise. Above all be reliable. If you and your friend agree to meet somewhere, keep appointments, don't be late, and do not stand him or her up. If you are not going to make it on time, call them as soon as you realize it. Apologize and ask for a reschedule. Don't make them wait for you unexpectedly; it's rude and is certainly not a good way to keep a potential friendship. When you say you will do something, do it. Be someone people know they can count on

BE A GOOD LISTENER: *(Job 33: 1 -7)*: Job's friend, Elihu, persuaded him to give a patient hearing. There are four stages of listening which are: i) Hearing, ii) Attention, iii) Understanding, iv) Remembering.

Effective listening begins by giving your attention to what is being said by your friend. If you feel superior to your friend, you may find yourself not really listening to what they say. If you are in hurry or have your mind on another matter, you may hear words and even answer without really listening. Many people think that in order to be seen as "friend material" they have to appear very interesting. Far more important than this, however, is the ability to listen carefully to what people say, remember important details about them (e.g. their names, families, strengths, weaknesses, likes and dislikes), ask questions about their interests, and take the time to learn more about them. You don't want to be the person that always has a better story than anyone else, or breaks off the conversation instead of continuing the flow of it. If you want to be a good listener follow these rules; i) concentrate your mental energies on listening, ii) show interest and alertness with your body and eyes, iii) be patient with the friend, iv) do not act as though you are in a hurry, v) try to discern what type of response they expect, vi) help or simply give assurance and caring, even though you are in a hurry, vii) not to interrupt or show disagreement until your friend has completed their message.

KNOWING A PERSON COMPLETELY:

"Then the sailors said to each other 'Come, and let us cast lots to find out that is responsible for making this entire calamity.' They cast lots and the lot fell on Jonah. So they asked him, 'Tell us, who are responsible for making this trouble for us? What do you do? Where do you come from? What is your country? From what people are you' He answered, 'I am a Hebrew and I worship the Lord, the God of heaven, who made the sea and the land?" (Jonah 1: 7- 9)

It is appropriate to fully know the nature, character, work and background of the person you choose to be your friend. Biblically, the ship crew in; *Jonah 1: 6-9;* only found the solution to the raging storm when they sought to know more about Jonah. It was only then they were able to help save the lives of the others on the ship, and Jonah also realized that God wanted him to take the task set before him. I believe the questions that were posed to Jonah pricked his conscience so much, that he had no alternative but to heed to the voice of God. In like manner, guilty individuals must be interrogated and known before being accepted as friends. We should likewise bring strangers under serious cross-examination before accepting their company or friendship. It is only by doing this that you can decide to trust the person or forget his companionship. This produces the power of union, which leads to trust and true friendship. Many are willing to make friends but are not willing to reveal their true identity to us. A friend, who knows all he has to know about his friends will not mind sharing his poverty, persecution, glories and triumphs with them.

KNOWING PEOPLE: What is more important than knowing people who matter to us most? The number of such people may not be very high, yet they influence our lives completely. If we can know the minds and thoughts of such people, there is no doubt that we not only make our life better, but also the lives of people around us. It is no secret that we can get what we want in life only by proper understanding of others. We can bring peace and happiness to others only by understanding each other, though understanding is the most difficult part of friendship. This knowledge is not taught in any school or college. Our understanding of man is based on the intellectual knowledge derived from the books of psychology, management, religion or culture, etc, but these fail to help us in real life. Which theory is to be applied to a person, when every person is uniquely different and every theory is different? The question is; are there really methods of getting to know a person so completely?

ONE PERSON, FOUR PERSONALITIES: We all wear many hats in our life. We are the simplest creatures on earth yet at the same time the most complex beings. Who are we? We are different persons in different environments. We may be simple people while at home, who our children relate with being our children. We play with them, enjoy the simple games and become childlike to meet their standards and appeal. However, our education, professions and knowledge do not sometimes influence, especially, children, because they are in a world of their own and we need to step down to enjoy their company.

We also exhibit different personalities when we are with our friends. They also know us in a different way from our children. They are able to fit into our educational circle better because we may have read the same courses or attended the same schools. We are able to read well into their minds as we know the minds of all our friends, because we can tell when they are in a good or bad mood. The older the friendship, the better our understanding becomes. Friends not only know our personality but also become an integral part of our personality. After all, it is wisely said, *'A man is known by the company he keeps.'* Thus, your friends are often an indication of your personality.

We are again a different personality while at work with colleagues. Your friend here is not viewed as friends, because as far work is concerned, professionalism and performance are what matter and not friendship. Even when you are the boss, you must make sure you put the friendship aside and make sure your friend works the way they are supposed to. Our actions and thoughts are shaped by our job structure.

Finally, we are part of a society, nation and the world at large. Everything that happens in the world, I.e. global warming, homosexuality, child abuse, floods, and so on, has an effect on us. The happenings in the twenty-first century are different from those of the tenth century. However, man is not merely a body, i.e. a material entity, but also comprises a mind, soul and spirit. The complete personality of the person can be known only by knowing his body, mind, soul and spirit. Once you know all four, there is nothing left in the person to be known, as they have become your extended self by the presence of a common spirit. The entity of body is known by sight, touch and smell, but the methods to know the other three aspects of man include:

i. THE MENTAL SELF: The mind of the person is the most important attribute in his or her professional life. The mind of the person is shaped by the quality of their education and experience in life. One can know the mind of a person from the person's educational qualification and professional experience. The mind is the source of reason and logic applied by them while interacting with the world. One can also understand the mind of a person in the course of discussion and communication, e.g. by the way they respond to logic and reasoning.

ii. INTELLECTUAL SELF: The body, sense and mind are independent of each other. It is also possible to measure these attributes of the human personality by the use of instruments or tests. Yet they are all controlled by the soul of a person, which represents the intelligence of that person. The mind and body are not static but dynamic. A person is happy in one situation but can get worried at the very next moment. A person may be active in one moment but may become inactive in another maybe, due to illness, hunger or tiredness a few moments later. Thus, our assessment of a person may be totally wrong if it is based merely on the knowledge of the physical and mental self.

The senses are superior to the body. Beyond the sense is the mind, beyond the mind is the soul (individual intelligence) and beyond the soul is God (universal Intelligence) . Knowing the 'self intelligence' of the person is, therefore, extremely important as it changes over time. Just as one knows the name of a tree from the fruit it bears, it is intelligence which controls the body and the mind. If a person speaks evil of everybody, it shows that his core intelligence is evil.

The Lord Jesus said;

"Watch out for false prophets. They come to you in sheep's clothing, but inwardly they are ferocious wolves. By their fruit you will recognize them. Do people pick grapes from thorn bushes, or figs from thistles? Likewise every good tree bears good fruit, but a bad tree bears bad fruit. A good tree cannot bear bad fruit, and a bad tree cannot bear good fruit. Every tree that does not bear good fruit is cut down and thrown into the fire, thus, by their fruit you will recognize them." (Matthew 7: 15–20)

KNOW THE TREE: People are able to recognize a tree not by its leaves, or flowers, but by the kind of fruit it bears. The flower may be beautiful with a great and delicate scent, but these are merely 'embellishments.' It is the *"Fruit"* that is of great value to man. A person's personality may be fair as meets the human eye, but the conduct or lifestyle (fruit) determines the nature of his actions. Many people today exhibit different characters at home, work and church etc. Some people also have false character, and act with pretence and are fast to deceive others. Beware of such people, have nothing to do with them. Guard against such temptation. Some outwardly appear innocent, harmless, and meek just to be accepted as friends. Such people easily deceive, manipulate and cause great harm to you when you least expect; they are sheep in wolf's clothing. A person with good fruit does not need to convince anyone to come close to them or to trust them. To know if a person is good and qualify as a friend, observe that person's lifestyle. A good person's character promotes charity, humility, and piety with others; such people are not proud, contentious, and uncharitable and the other negative attributes one can think of.

'The worthlessness of a tree calls for its removal from the orchard lest it infects the others.'
The real nature of a person is the entire intelligence level of that person. Body and mind are merely the tools used in controlling the intelligence of the self. Just like fire can be used to cook food or burn things, the body and mind are also used for good and bad purposes. The intelligence of a person has to be understood by the synthesis of the diverse traits and actions of the person using our own intelligence and reasoning.

iii. THE SPIRITUAL SELF: It is believed in scripture and by philosophers that every living being has the spark of the Spirit of God in them. No person is, therefore, independent of other beings as the common thread of this spirit connects everyone together. It is due to that common spirit we cry when we see people suffering and rejoice with those who are rejoicing. It is due to the spiritual self that we connect ourselves with the rest of the world. The spiritual self of a person is the non-material aspect of a person's personality. It is best known to our loved ones when there are no material rewards or punishment for our actions. In our homes, we get no reward or punishment for being nice or nasty to our children, wives or parents. Yet the expression of our spiritual self is a pivotal part of all our happiness and pain.

A spiritual person, therefore, highly values the non-material realities of life and seeks happiness in selfless activities. We are all spiritual to some extent and also get happy at times. Wealth cannot feel any happiness because it has no spirit, soul or reasoning. It is only man that can feel happiness when he acquires wealth since he can use the wealth for important and beneficial gains. The understanding of the spiritual self is purely based on intuition and requires no knowledge or reasoning. It is similar to the understanding that a child has about his or her parents. The signs of spirituality include peace, love and joy. When you meet a person and feel peaceful, loving and happy, that person is likely to be spiritual. You can, therefore, expect compassion from such a person. If the feeling is anything other than what I have stated, you are with a materialist and potentially devilish person.

THE COMPLETE KNOWLEDGE OF A PERSON: It is only by the knowledge of these four aspects of a person, that you can understand the real being of that person. Such an understanding of a person requires not only the logical reasoning, but also the use of basic instinct, intelligence, intuition and experience.

MY FRIEND'S SECRET:

So Delilah said to Samson, "Tell me the secret of your great strength and how you can be tied up and subdued. How can you say, 'I love you,' when you won't confide in me? This is the third time you have made a fool of me and haven't told me the secrets of your great strength.' So he told her everything. 'No razor has ever been used on my head,' he said, 'because I have been a Nazirite, set apart to God since birth. If my head were shaved, my strength would leave me, and I would become as weak as any other man." (Judges 16: 1–17)

The Philistines, whom were enemies of Samson, employed Delilah, his 'so-called friend', to reveal the secret behind his unusual strength to her. After Samson had revealed his secret to Delilah, she, in turn, told his enemies, who then captured and defeated him. We must learn to keep our secrets from some 'so-called friends'. It is unwise to tell that which could destroy you to so-called friends. Samson let out his secret and it was used against him. One of the best things about having a friend is that you have someone to whom you can talk to about anything, even secrets that you hide from the rest of the world. The key to being a good confidante (a person to whom secrets are entrusted) is the ability to keep secrets. Before you open up to people, build up trust and make sure you can confide in them. Learn also to be honest with yourself and the secrets of others. When you hear rumors about the people you call friends, never be quick to join in the gossip or condemn them, because this is the time for you to show your commitment to your friendship.

HE COMES WITH A GOSSIP: Gossiping, has become accepted even by Christians, to be part of human life. No sir, gossiping to destroy the image of a person is an abomination! When you sit with people and gossip about another person, take note that those same people will gossip about you in your absence.

"You shall not go up and down as a gossiper among your people." (Leviticus. 19: 18)

It is a great offense to spread a secret committed to you in confidence to another person. A friend of a faithful spirit proves himself to be firm and true by keeping secrets from the knowledge and power of another. Secret revealers are called *'Newsmongers.'* They will tell even their own secrets, rather than say nothing. One has to be on one's guard against confiding in such people. It is said that one can share any secret with a true friend without fears. A friend may know your deepest fears and weaknesses and yet will never take advantage them. However, keeping a friend's secret(s) to yourself and not telling the world about them is what builds up and makes the bond of friendship strong and long-lasting. You need to develop trust and mutual understanding before you start sharing secrets with each other.

A SECRET IS NOT A JOKE: There is a phase in a person's life, especially from teenage years, when he or she starts to have a personal periphery in life, which parents are excluded from. The reason is simple; they know and believe that there are some things that their friends understand better concerning them than their parents can ever do. In such cases they entrust their secrets in the hands of their friends rather than their parents. There are friends who are able to conceal our secrets better than even close relations. There is a general notion that females are the best secret sharers. What such people fail to understand is that males also have secrets, which they share on their own. Personally, I am of the view that males are good at keeping secrets of their friends because they talk less, unlike their female counterparts. It is prudent to know that every human being has the potential of keeping or revealing a secret. We all have something that is so dear to our hearts that we have kept at heart or have entrusted to a friend. Secrets are not limited only to teenagers! Secrets can be shared at any age and there is absolutely no such hard and fast rule about that. Sharing secrets with your friend(s) is not just for fun or a silly joke; it also helps to develop a lasting and helpful relationship.

Who is your friend? With whom do you share your secrets? Do not disclose anything immediately first test your friend, by sharing just little secrets to see how they handle that information. In doing this, make sure that what you reveal cannot be used against you, or another person. Do not ever reveal a secret which may be used in hurting you, or another person to a new and untested friend.

CHAPTER 3

THE JOY OF FRIENDSHIP

Is there anything in the world purer than unselfish friendship? Yet it is the thing we take so little pain to cultivate and keep. Friendship is often the only thing many people abuse through neglect. One reason why so many people have so few friends is that they have so little to give, and yet they expect so much. If you develop attractive and lovable qualities, friends will come around you. Most of us attend to everything else first, and if we have any little scraps of time left we give them to our friends, when, we ought to make a business of our friendships. Are they worth it? Is there anything more beautiful in this world than the consciousness of having sweet, helpful friends, whose commitment is not affected in any way by the difficulties you are going through; friends who love us even more in suffering than in prosperity? Cicero put it this way:

'They seem to take away the sun from the world, those who withdraw friendship from life.
There is no helpmeet (helpmate) or joy-giver like a true friend!'

Who's Your Friend?

OUT FOR OUR INTEREST: It means a great deal to have fervent true friends always looking out for our best interests, working for us all the time, saying a good word for us at every opportunity, supporting us and speaking out for us in our absence, when we need a friend. Protecting our "easily offend" areas of life, weak spots, stopping gossips, killing lies which would destroy our names and it continues, correcting false impressions, trying to set us right, overcoming the dangers created by some mistakes or, some first bad impression we made in some foolish moment. They are always doing something to give us a lift or help us along. We can talk with true friends about every facet of life; our joys, trials, triumphs, tragedies, hopes, wants and needs. We can make ourselves vulnerable to them, knowing they will always think and act in our interests. True friends are favour to us. Oh, what a blessing our friends are to our weaknesses, our shortcoming, disabilities and our failures or temporary defeats. How out of love, they cover our faults, and our imperfections. What a cold and empty world this would be without our friends, those who believe in us, even when everybody else rejects us, those who love us, not for what we have, but for what and who we are! Friends who appreciate us, who help us build up instead of destroying our self-confidence, double our power of accomplishment. In their presence we feel strong and equal to almost any duty. Our friends, if they be many can add more to the riches and happiness of our existence.

MOST TOUCHING THING: Our best friends never embarrass us by making us feel inferior or weak. On the other hand, they always give us a lift upward, a push onward. What a difference a true friend has made in the lives of most of us. How many a strong, true friendship has kept from hopelessness, from giving up the struggle for success! How many men and women have been kept from suicide by the thought that someone loved them, believed in them; how many have preferred to suffer torture and maltreatment rather than dishonoring or disappointing their friends. I agree with the statement that if at the end of life we can count at least two people who are true friends who were willing to do anything for us at the drop of a hat, who stand ready when we are hurting or need help, we are indeed rich and fortunate. One of the most touching things I know of, is the office of a real friend to one who is not a friend to him or herself; one who has lost their self-respect, self-control and fallen to the level of being 'nobody'. This is friendship, indeed, which will stand by us when we will not stand by ourselves. I know a man who stood by a friend who had become such a slave to drinking and all sorts of vice, that even his family had turned him out of doors. When his father and mother, wife and children had forsaken him, his friend remained true. He would follow him through nights in his drunkenness, and many a time saved him from freezing to death, when he was so intoxicated that he could not stand. Many times this friend would leave his home and hunt in the slums for him, to keep him from the hand of the police or criminals, to protect him from the cold when everyone else had forsaken him; and this great love and commitment finally saved the 'poor alcoholic friend' and sent him back to the comfortable manner of life and to his home. Can any money measure the value of such friendship! Who is your friend?

TELL THE TRUTH; *"Friends deceive friends, and no one speaks the truth." (Jeremiah 9: 5)*

Who's Your Friend?

Many people have made themselves masters of the art of lying to their friends. The friendship which shrinks from telling the truth is not true friendship. No great friendship can rest upon hypocrisy and lies. Sincerity is the very heart of friendship e.g. Let us imagine a women we know has gained excess weight, many of us would lie and say "No, you're in great shape, you look great", but knowing the truth that they had gained weight which was noticeable. A true friend should tell the truth even if it hurts, but say it in love. Many people seem to think that friends are mere incidental things in life, and it is not worthwhile to put oneself out a great deal to labour and care for them by pointing out the truth to them. Do not be afraid to tell your friends that you love them. Tell them of the qualities you admire in them. Also, tell them of the vices you dislike in them. Do not presume too much upon your friendships. It is good for us to be reproved, and told our faults, by our friends. If true love in the heart has but zeal and courage enough to show itself in dealing plainly with our friend, and reproving them for what they say and do wrong, this is really better than secret hated. ***(Leviticus 19: 17)***

Secret love that does not show itself in good fruits to our friends and neighbors, but compliments them in the sins and faults to prejudice their soul is no love. Faithful are the reproofs or corrections of a friend. Though for the present they are as painful as wounds, it is a sign that our friends are faithful indeed, if in love to our souls, they will not permit evil upon us, nor let us alone in it. The physician's care is to cure the patient's disease, not to please his palate.

FRIENDSHIP AND ADMIRATION: Friendship rests largely on admiration, while admiration is that which is admired or excites approval. Many are not capable of forming great friendship because they do not have the qualities themselves, which attract noble qualities in others. If you are packed together with vice, you cannot expect anyone to admire you. If you are without love and patience or you lack the ability to give, also if you are not broad-minded and sympathetic, you cannot expect that good-hearted and noble characters to surround you.

"Tell me who admires you and loves you, and I will tell you who you are."
(Charles Augustin Sante-Beuve 1804-1869 French literature critic)

Having a happy temperament, a desire to give joy and gladness and to be helpful to everyone, are wonderful aids to friendship. The capacity for friendship is the great test of character. Bad people cannot keep a friendship; people who lack trust cannot keep true friendship. Friends become false if they cannot show their true colors. We only reap what we have sown with our friends and the harvest is the friendship. If the seed is poor, the harvest will be poor. The man who is rich in friendship has sown richly with sympathy, patience, love, interest, helpfulness, and admiration. Seneca said, "The purpose of friendship is to have one dearer to me than myself." In friendship lies a road to happiness. But you will also find some friends insincere, and friendship but a name. You will suffer deception, but never mind, keep to your own course of being a true friend, knowing that in a true friend, worthy of true friendship, lies the road to real lasting happiness.

FRIENDSHIP AND TRANSPARENCY: Transparency is an inherent and integral characteristic of a good friend. It is closely linked to the quality of communication. In fact transparency strengthens communication. Transparency is the quality in which friends are able to expose themselves in full measure, without any reservation, in a manner that friends understand and get to know them through and through. This, in order words, is unveiling oneself to others and letting the mask fall. The extent, to which one unveils oneself unreservedly, willingly and sincerely, shows the degree of reality and the quality of transparency.

I personally like what Shakira the famous pop singer was quoted to have said;

"It doesn't bother me to talk about my private life; it doesn't bother me to say anything. My life is like a glass of water, transparent."

It means there is absolutely nothing that a true friend wants to cover up and has the full intention of exposing themselves. In this quality the friend admits to all, what he is inside and outside. True friends must exercise this quality gradually, progressively, purposefully and fully in order to be meaningful to each other. It is a special property of personality that no one outside of you should know you until you expose yourself to him or her. Any unveiling, therefore, which is not exposing oneself is not truly unveiling. When a friend does not show exactly who they truly are, is not demonstrating transparency but a covering up. Many of us go around wearing a mask. Why are we afraid to let others know who we really are? We are afraid to be transparent, because we fear others may not like what they see and reject us. No one really likes wearing a mask. We need friendship with someone from whom there is nothing to hide; that is a true friend.

LOVERS SEEK PRIVACY: Transparency with God is the foundation for inter-personal transparency.

Friendship arises when two or more discover that they have some insight or interest in common. Lovers seek privacy. True friendship seeks transparency. The very condition of having a friend is that we should want something else besides friendship. Where the truthful answer to the question *'Do you see the same truth?"* would be *'I don't care about the truth I only want you to be my friend.'* No friendship can simply arise. It must be about something, even if it were only a mutual enthusiasm for dominoes or white mice. Those who have nothing can share nothing; those who are going nowhere can have no fellow travelers.

'If you find a person with a common commitment to a deeply-held truth or passion, and if you then provide mutual transparency and consistency, you have a developing friendship.' The person who wants to shut up and hideaway his inner life from others, and who enjoys being alone having personal privacy, or who wants to be a recluse should not enter into friendship. Such a person may have fans or admire others, but he cannot reproduce himself in others through transparency. Reproducing oneself and building up others are the basis of friendship.

CHAPTER 4

WHAT DOES THE BIBLE SAY?
ABOUT FRIENDSHIP?

The Lord Jesus Christ gives us the definition of a true friend in the book of John:

"Greater proof of love has no man than this that a man lay down his life for his friend. You are friends, if you do whatever I command you. Henceforth I call you not servants; for the servant knows not what his lord does: but I have called you friends; for all things that I have heard of my Father I have made known to you." (John 15: 13-15)

The Lord Jesus Christ is the real example of a true friend, for He laid down His life for His 'Friends'. Moreover, 'whosoever will' may become His friend by trusting in Him as their personal Saviour, being born again and receiving new life through and In Him. Jesus called His disciples friends, because He treated them as friends. He revealed His mind and heart to them; made known His plans; told them about His death, His resurrection and ascension. He did not keep His friends in the dark. He is an example to emulate if you want to be called a true friend; the genuine proof of true friendship. There should be free, unrestrained fellowship among friends. A friend who gives his life gives all, and could give more.

JESUS AND FRIENDSHIP: Jesus also gives another parable about true friendship:

"And he said to them, which of you shall have a friend, and shall go to him at midnight, and say to him, friend, lend me three loaves; for a friend of mine in his journey is come to me, and I have nothing to set before him? And he from within shall answer and say, trouble me not: the door is now shut, and my children are with me in bed; I cannot rise and give you. I say to you, though he will not rise and give him, because he is his friend, yet because of his importunity, he will rise and give him as many as he needed." (Luke 11: 5-8)

The friend in the above parable needed assistance from his friend. He went to his friend at midnight, an unwholesome hour, and a time it would be most inconvenient for his friend to help him. This was because his friend would naturally be in bed and his house shut. Yet, if the friend had travelled on foot all day, and did not arrive until midnight, he must definitely have been very hungry. Hospitality demands that our friends or neighbours be taken care of, no matter when they call for help. *"For a friend of mine in his journey is come to me"* this makes the case more urgent. This is a strong reason why the friend should have prompt relief. Suppose a friend, upon a sudden emergency, comes to ask for your help at an odd time or without an appointment, not for himself, but for his neighbour that visits unexpectedly; would you assist them or turn him or her away? What would your response be? A true friend would be moved to accommodate him.

JONATHAN AND DAVID: A further example of true friendship is the relationship that existed between David and Saul's son, Jonathan. Jonathan stood by his friend David in spite of Saul's pursuit of David and attempts to kill. The Bible records that:

"When David had finished speaking to Saul, the soul of Jonathan was knit with the soul of David, and Jonathan loved him as his own life. Jonathan made a covenant with David, because he loved him as his own life. And Jonathan stripped himself of the robe that was on him and gave it to David, and his amour, even his sword, his bow and his belt." (1 Samuel 18: 1-4)

The bond of friendship which Jonathan formed with David was an evidently true friendship. David was later anointed to take the crown out of Saul's hands and over Jonathan's head. Yet Jonathan, the natural heir to his father's throne, entered into a covenant with David. God so ordered it, that David's way might be the clearer with his 'rival' as his friend. Jonathan demonstrated an extraordinary kindness and affection for him. He declared his love to David through generous gifts. He was uneasy at seeing so great a soul, though lodged in so fair a body, disguised in the mean and despicable dress of a shepherd, therefore decided to clothe him in princely robes by giving the robe that was his. Jonathan stripped himself of his robe and sword and dressed David in them. They had similar bodily features, a coincidence, that enhanced the stableness of their minds. David seen in Jonathan's clothes, looked very much like Jonathan's twin brother. What a blessing to their great friendship! They cemented their friendship constantly by entering into a godly covenant with each other.

True friendship is constant. Those who treasure their friendship enjoy true fellowship. Jonathan and David found in each other the affection and true friendship they could not find in their own families. Jonathan, a prince, gave all the material gifts. David, the son of a poor man, gave love and respect. A man, who gets all but gives nothing does not understand true friendship. True friendship exchanges gifts. Love was constant between David and Jonathan; each was worthy of the other. They had a friendship which would not be affected by changes and chances, and which exemplified all that the ancients had said on the subject;

'Ten philian isotela einai kai main psuchen, ton heterm anton.' Translation: *'Friendship produces an entire sameness; it is one soul in two bodies; a friend is another self.'*

KING SOLOMON ON FRIENDSHIP: The book of Proverbs is another good source of wisdom regarding friendship.

"A friend loves at all times, and a brother is born for adversity." (Proverbs 17: 17)

A friend loves at all times. He or she is a faithful brother or sister in times of adversity or emergency. There should be no intervals of forgetfulness or alienation in true friendship. True friendship may deepen into a spiritual, moral brother and sisterhood if properly taken care of. A friend proves themselves true in times of need and can deepen further like the bond between real blood brothers or sisters. A friend is called 'a brother or sister', when they stick to a companion in extremely trying times. The wise King Solomon sums this up in the words;

"Faithful are the wounds of a friend; but the kisses of an enemy are deceitful." (Proverbs 27: 6)

It is dangerous to be caressed and flattered by an enemy, whose kisses are deceitful. We should take no pleasure in them because we can put no confidence in them. Example; the kisses of Joab and Judas were treacherous.
As Christians, we should be on our guard and refuse to be charmed by false friends. Rather, they are to be rejected. May the good Lord deliver us from the kisses of false friends, from lying lips and from a lying tongue? Flattery looks like friendship, just as a wolf looks like a dog.

ONE MAN IS NOBODY:

"Iron sharpens iron; so a man sharpens the countenance of his friend." (Proverbs 27: 17)

The significance of this proverb is well known in education. One man is nobody, neither will flipping through a book in the corner make one an accomplished student of human character. Wise, profitable discourse sharpens men's intellect, and those that have ever so much knowledge may, by conference, have something else added to them.

Pure discourse sharpens men's looks, cheers the spirit, puts liveliness into the countenance and makes men bright and fit for business, those who were rough, dull and inactive). We should be careful with who we choose as our friends or whom we converse with, because the influence upon us is great, either for the better or for the worst. True friends should not pass away time or ridicule one another, but rather provoke and encourage one another to love and good works and so make one another wiser and better. A steel knife will have a better edge when it is properly sharpened, so one friend may be the means of sharpening another.

'Ergo fungar vice cotis acutum, Redere quae feum valet exors ipsa secandi.'
Translation: *'But let me sharpen others as hone gives edge to razors, though it has none.'*

Two minds, thus acting on each other, become more acute. As the saying goes 'two minds are better than one'. A friend will sharpen the mind of his friend, by mutual conversation and godly instruction. Our lives brighten up in meeting intelligent friends, who sharpen the intellect and warm the heart. 'False friends are those who roll out the carpet for you one day and pull it out from under you the next day'. But a true friend will strengthen you with his prayers, bless you with his love, and encourage you with his hope.
Who is your friend?

THE AMOS PRINCIPLE:

"Can two walk together, unless they have agreed to do so?" (Amos 3: 3)

FRIENDS ARE OF LIKE MINDS: The truth that comes from all of this is friendship is a relationship that is entered into by individuals and it is only as good or as close as those individuals choose to make it. Where there is disagreement and no alignment, there can be no friendship. Two people at variance must first accommodate their differences before there can be any interchange of good office. Israel has affronted God; it has broken its covenant with Him, and yet expects to continue to walk with Him, without first seeking repentance and reformation of character for Him to turn away His anger. "But how can that be?" says God. You cannot expect a friend to walk and agree with you when you have differences and you do not agree on common things. We cannot expect that God would be present with, or act for us, unless we are reconciled to Him. You cannot expect that a friend would be present with or act in your favour, until you are reconciled to them. Friends who no longer agree can no longer walk together.

FRIENDSHIP WITH UNBELIEVERS: As Christians, we have to constantly face temptations and the attacks of the world around us. Everything we see, read, do, hear and put in our bodies etc, affects us in one way or another. That's why to maintain a close relationship with God; we have to put aside our old ways of doing things; the things we watch on the TV, old bad habits, e.g. excessive drinking, smoking, the activities we participate in, and the people we spend our time with. People are divided into only two categories, those who belong to the world and its ruler Satan, and those who belong to God. (Refer to Acts 26:18). Those two groups of people are described in terms of opposites throughout the Bible, i.e. those in darkness and those in the light; those with eternal life and those with eternal death; those who have peace with God and those who are at war with Him; those who believe the truth and those who believe lies; those on the narrow path to heaven and those on the broad road to destruction, and many more. Clearly, the message of Scripture is that believers are completely different from unbelievers, and it is from this perspective that we must discern what kind of friendship we can really have with unbelievers.

The book of proverbs has a few wise verses on believers befriending unbelievers:

"The righteous should choose his friend carefully, for the way of the wicked leads them astray." (Proverbs 12: 26)

"He who walks as (a companion) with wise men are wise, but he who associates with (self- confident) fools is a fool himself." (Proverbs 13: 20)

To walk with a person implies love and attachment; and it is impossible not to imitate those we walk with, so we say "Show me his company, and I will tell you the man. Let me know the company he keeps, and I shall easily guess his moral character".

"Do not make friends with an angry man, do not associate with one easily angered, or you may learn his ways and get yourself ensnared." (Proverbs 22: 24)

Furious spirit has a wonderful and unaccountable influence upon spirit. From those with whom we associate we acquire habits and practices, imbue their spirit, reflect their temperaments and walk in their steps. We cannot choose their company, for we may soon learn ways that will entrap our souls. Whosoever comes into a near relation with a passionate, furious man or woman easily accommodates themselves to their manners. Though we must be civil to all people, yet we must be careful whom we accept as a friend and contract a familiarity with. A person who is easily provoked, touchy, and apt to resent affronts others especially when in a passion as they care not what they say or do, but grow outrageous. Such a person is not fit to be made a friend or companion. Those who go with such a character are apt to grow with them. All these are people who have not been saved;

'Do not be yoked together with unbelievers. For what do righteousness and wickedness have in common? Or what fellowship can light have with darkness?' (2 Corinthians 6: 14)

KEEP IN GOOD COMPANY:

"Bad Company corrupts good character." (1 Corinthians 15: 33)

'There were two dry logs of wood, and a green lush log; but the dry logs burned up the green one'. There is no difficulty in this saying; "be not deceived; evil communication corrupts good manners."

'Communication' means; being together, having companionship and close contact, while sharing conversation. The meaning of this passage is to emphasize the contact with evil-minded men, or friendship and conversation with people who hold erroneous opinion(s), or with those who are impure in their lives, tends to corrupt the hearts and morals of others. Intimacy with the profligate

is apt to corrupt our pure principles. Those who want to keep their innocence must keep good company. You may be sound in the faith and have the life and the power of godliness, and at first frequent their company only for the sake of conversation, you may think your faith can protect you against their infidelity; but you will soon find your faith weakened by their glozed and flattering speech; and once you get under their empire of doubt, unbelief will soon prevail; their bad company will corrupt your morals; and their two dry logs will soon burn up your green log.

'*Phtheirousin eethe chreesth' homiliai kakai* ' translation: 'Bad company good moral corrupts.'

Christians are slaves to God. If we become deeply involved, either in platonic or romantic relations with non-Christians, we are setting ourselves up for trouble. It can, and often does cause the Christian to stumble in their walk with God, and fall back into a sinful life, also turns others away from God by misrepresenting God and Christianity.
Another detrimental effect of closeness with unbelievers is our tendency to water down the truth of scripture, so as to not offend them. There are difficult truths in the word of God, truth such as judgment and Hades (hell). When we trivialize or ignore these doctrines, or try to 'soft pedal' them, we are in essence, calling God a liar for the sake of those already in the grasp of the enemy (Satan). Although these close friendships are not recommended, it does not, however, mean we should turn our back on and ignore unbelievers either, as it is our fair duty and responsibility to continue Jesus' mission to witness and give testimony and spread the gospel.

SYMPATHIZING WITH THE IGNORANT:

"He must be kind to everyone and mild-tempered; he must be a skilled and suitable teacher, patient and forbearing and willing to suffer wrong." (2 Timothy 2: 24)

A servant of the Lord should be a man or woman of peace. They should not indulge in the feelings which commonly give rise to conflict or fighting. They should act as in all cases, with a kind spirit, and a mild temper; with nothing designed to provoke and irritate their fellow human; so that whatever may be the result of a discussion, 'the bond of peace.' As a Christian you must be sensitive of your own ignorance, therefore, able to sympathise with those who are ignorant even as you seem to be hemmed in by your own weaknesses. We should make allowance for unbelievers to come near us. The Lord Jesus Christ allowed sinful men into His presence. Let us have compassion on those who are guilty of sin(s). We should find a place in our hearts to pity and love them, and intercede with God for them. The great majority of the human race offends God through ignorance and weakness. The word instructs us to have compassion on the ignorant by showing them the way out. Christ loved us while we were sinners, so believers in Christ should love unbelievers until they come to faith and believe. We should gently teach those who oppose the truth, and be patient with difficult people.

'Let your good deeds shine out for all to see, so that everyone will praise your heavenly Father.'

We should serve unbelievers so they may see God through us and turn to Him in praise. There is great power in the prayer of a righteous person, so bring your concern for unbelievers before God and He will listen. Many have been saved because of the intercession of prayer and service of Christians, so don't turn your back on unbelievers, though having any kind of intimate relations with an unbeliever can quickly and easily turn into something that is a hindrance to your walk with Christ. We are called to evangelize the lost, not to be intimate with them. There is nothing wrong with building quality friendship with unbelievers, but the primary focus of such relationships should be to win them to Christ by sharing the gospel with them and demonstrating God's saving power in our lives.

JOB'S FRIENDS: The book of Job presents the story of a man who lost his family, his health, and his great wealth in a severe test of suffering. Job was not meant to know the explanation for his suffering; and on this simple fact everything hangs. If Job had known, there would have been no place for faith in God.

'Behind a frowning situation, God hides a smiling face.'

The centre-problem was: Why did Job suffer? He was a man of unquestionable character and faith, who trusted God with his heart and life. This necessarily involves the question of human suffering as a whole. Job's three friends seek to explain Job's case by their own understanding in general. The results were far from satisfactory. Take first Job's friends; Eliphaz the Temanite, Bildad the Shuhite, and Zophar the Naamathite. They came from far to console Job; but they all came to the same conclusion; that Job must have brought all of this on himself. They believed that he must have committed some hidden sins and his only way out was to 'get right' with God. And as the dialogue developed, their condoling turned to condemnation.

ELIPHAZ: (Meaning: God is fine gold). To begin with, let us glance quickly through the character and speech of Eliphaz, the eldest and the wisest. Eliphaz is the first of Job's friends to speak. He based his argument on experience. He examined Job's former lifestyle, and then declared what he has learned by observation, that suffering is always the direct outcome of sin, and God's judgment on it. He drew this hard and fast conclusion about his friend, Job, that he was, in reality, a hypocrite and that is why he was suffering. This is a friend of a fixed and rigid nature, who lacked the ability to comfort a friend in difficult and tough times. Eliphaz was a religious moralist. A man who's belief was to control the morals of others by placing censorship. Most of his speech to Job was judgmental. Thus, many readers think that Eliphaz, Job's so called friend, was either a false friend or a miserable comforter.

IN DIFFICULT SITUATIONS: When you think about it, Eliphaz was in a difficult situation. He was the first to speak to a friend whose world had collapsed and was suffering considerable physical and mental pain. How do you approach such a person? Do you say you are sorry? That might sound common, or do you launch right into what you want to say? That might be or sound insensitive. Maybe, try to say something to identify with your friend? But the falseness of your approach would be plain to see. It takes great wisdom, understanding and love to handle a friend in difficult moments.

Eliphaz does the best he can and changes his way of approach and handles Job (His Friend) in a friendly way. This is what he says:

"If someone ventures a word with you, will you be impatient? But who can keep from speaking?" (Job 4: 2)

Eliphaz was superior to the others with discernment and consideration for people. As a friend he did not begin to speak merely by making a speech, but professed that he would not have spoken, if he had not been pressed by the importance of the subject, and had not been full of matter. To a great extent, this is a good rule to adopt, by not making speeches, unless there are feelings which weigh up the mind. As a friend, it is also proper not to pretend in difficult matters, but only allow what may be said or done. You ought to be afraid of grieving, especially In front of that friend who is already in suffering, least you add pain to his or her pain.

"The longer I live, the longer allowance I make for human infirmities." said John Wesley.

BILDAD: (Meaning; Bel has loved). Bildad and other friends of Job came to see him, and they all sympathized with his suffering, and stayed with him for seven days and seven nights. However, they all came to the same conclusion; that Job must have brought all of this on himself. Bildad was particularly sure of this as we are told in his self-righteous lecture to Job;

"Then Bildad the Shuhite replied, 'How long will you say such things? Your words are a blustering wind. Does God

pervert justice? When your children sinned against Him, He gave them over to the penalty of their sin. But if you will look to God and plead with the Almighty, if you are pure and upright, even now He will rouse Himself on your behalf and restore you to your rightful place." (Job 8: 1-6)

Bildad's argument is based on the supposition that God would deal with people in this life according to their character; and thus he infers that his friend Job has been guilty of some great wickedness; that punishment should come upon him in this manner. Friends should not think or argue in this way when sudden suffering and pains comes upon others. Nothing could be more unjust and severe, than to take it for granted that Bildad was a legalistic friend. Legalism sometimes can take a friend too far and to the extreme, and that is to neglect your obligation to love your fellow man. Bildad thinks he knows all about Job's relationship with God. The truth is that Job is a believer who is far more advanced in his spiritual life than Bildad, but Bildad doesn't know that, and in his ignorance he calls Job godless and carnal.

JOB NEEDS COMFORT: Bildad got it all wrong and misjudged God, and judged Job as a hypocrite; Job did not need judgment at this time, but comfort, care and love. As the saying goes, 'With this kind of friend, who needs enemies.' You don't need an enemy if you have such a legalistic, inconsiderate person for a friend. Who is you friend? Job has come close to despair and is beginning to think that things are hopeless, but Bildad is having none of it. He is a legalist, and believes the only reason Job is suffering is because he is being disciplined and punished by God. He believes everything that is going wrong in Job's life is his own fault, so it is time for Job to stop complaining. Little does Bildad know that Job is being given the opportunity to glorify God in the 'historical trial' of divine conflict! It is easy to have tolerant friends when times are good. It is only in really difficult times that you discover who your true friends are. So, ask yourself; who is your friend?

ZOPHAR: (Meaning 'Perhaps'). Zophar was an intolerant man. He possessed the spirit of unwillingness to recognize and respect differences in opinions and beliefs. He was a dogmatist who believed that argument had the power to establish things. This story brings to mind a verse in the Apocrypha's book of wisdom which says:

'A friend cannot be known in prosperity: and an enemy cannot be hidden in adversity'.

No truer example of this can be found than in the treatment of Job by this so -called friend, 'Zophar'. This is a friend who is content with mere assumption. He assumes and speaks with finality without consideration. This is a friend whose words have no evidence of reasoning. Zophar was rigid in speech and action, so much that he could not console his friend Job. Rigid-spirited friends should learn how to be patient and sensitive to friends specially while in a low state of mind. Zopha's rigid approach made him condemn Job. It takes love, patience and meekness to deal with a friend going through depression. Some friends often mistake the dictates of passion to be reason, therefore think they do well to be angry. So, again ask yourself; who is your friend?

ELIHU: (Meaning, 'He is my God or He remains my God and never change'). The above mentioned three friends of job have one and the same voice; that Job's suffering was the outcome of sin. But Elihu came with a new voice, a new approach, a new answer and a new appeal. He is a much younger man than the others, but rich in compassion and wisdom. The other three friends of Job came as accusers; Elihu came as a concerned friend who cared for the lowly. Eliphaz, Bildad and Zophar had wished to be judges; but Elihu would be a brother. He would seek and sit with his friend Job, in the fellowship of friendly sympathy, yet at the same time speak the real truth from God's side. What Job lacked at this time was an interpreter; it seems clear that Elihu considered himself to be the required interpreter to tell the meaning of Job's suffering. Elihu told Job that his suffering was 'educational', and that God is dealing with him in some higher matters. This is a friend who sees a different purpose in the suffering from that which other rigid and inconsiderate friends had seen. Elihu said, "Suffering is not exclusively punitive; it is corrective. It is not penal; it is moral. It does not only come to requite a man; it comes to restore a man".

CORRECTIVE SPIRIT: Eliphar, Bildad and Zophar had insisting on some supposed wicked behavior of Job's past. Elihu does not discuss whether Job has committed a grievous sin in the past. He accepts Job's protestation of innocence, and his point is simply that although Job's protestation of innocence may be genuine enough, his present attitude and spirit were wrong. Elihu as a good friend demonstrated a corrective and educative spirit rather than one of judicial and punitive. What a gracious and caring friend. Elihu was a friend with the heart of love, who would not afflict a friend in pain, but rather patiently accept, care, love and encouragement, no matter his condition. Who is your friend? Elihu was a reliable friend. He was an angel, a mediator and one of the thousands who spoke to Job words of encouragement. It takes love, patience and meekness to deal with a depressed friend. Some friends often mistake the dictates of the passion, and therefore think they do well to be angry.

'No one is useless who lightens the burden of another.'

WHY JOB'S FRIENDS CAME:

"When Job's friends, Eliphaz the Temanite, Bildad the Shuhite and Zophar the Naamathite, heard about all the troubles that had come upon him, they set out from their homes and met together by agreement to go and sympathize with him and to comfort him." (Job 2: 11)

The news of Job's extraordinary troubles soon spread far and wide. Some, who were his enemies, rejoiced over his troubles. But his friends concerned themselves with his troubles, and tried to comfort him. Job, in his prosperity had contracted friendship with many people. If they were his equals, he was not envious and if inferior to him, he had no disdain for them. Much of the comfort of this life lies in acquaintance and friendship with the prudent and virtuous. Although, these friends were harsh and hard, they yet continued their friendship with Job during his difficult moments, when most of his friends had forsaken him. (Job 19 vs. 14) If you have such friends you should value them highly!

THEY SAT WITH HIM: Job's three friends came, not to satisfy their curiosity on account of his troubles and the strangeness of his circumstances, but to mourn with him, to mingle their tears with his, and to comfort him. It is much more pleasant to visit our friends in affliction to whom comfort belongs than those to whom we must first speak conviction. Good friends should make appointments among themselves for doing good, so exciting and binding one another to their friendship, and assisting and encouraging one another in it. For carrying out good plans, let's join hands. Friends that aim well do well. The visit of Job's friends was not a brief visit; just to look at him and be gone; but as friends who would find no peace should they depart to their various homes, while their friend was in so much pain. So they resolved to stay with him until he was better. They stayed with and heard him out, though he could not entertain them as he would in happier days.

'Nullu ad amissas ibit amicus opes';
Translation: ***Those who have lost their wealth are not to expect the visit of their friends.'***

Job's friends were of diverse temperaments, yet they sat with him. Let us sit with our friends in difficult times, for such is friendship. Who is your friend and do they need your support at this time?

FRIENDSHIP AND COMFORT: To 'comfort' means to help make a sufferer a strong fortress emotionally or spiritually. To comfort is to intensely strengthen a sufferer so that the person can withstand attacks or endure conflicts. Job's friends came to help strengthen him on the inside to be able to endure the loss of his wealth, the death of his ten children, and the disease of his body, as well as all the mental and emotional pains that came with his condition.

The scripture makes it clear that Job's friends, though sitting with him for seven days, failed to comfort his suffering. They failed so badly that in ***Job 16: 2;*** Job says of them, ***"Miserable comforters are you all."*** Miserable comforters are also called burdensome friends, who irritate rather than comfort. Friends should not be only careful about their own comfort and welfare, but should also promote the comfort and welfare of their friends and all other people.

It was Cain that said; *" Am I my Brother's keeper?"* Friends must be carriers of one another's burdens, and so fulfill the law of Christ.

"And many of the Jews came to Mary and Martha to comfort them at the loss of their brother." (John 11: 19)

Mary and Martha were almost overwhelmed with sorrow at the death of their brother, but many of their Jewish friends came to comfort them. Where there are mourners, there should be comforters. It is a duty we owe to our friends in sorrow and pain to mourn with them and to comfort them, by mourning with them. It is of great importance to ensure that our friends in affliction are supported and comforted.

STRANGERS TO SUFFERING: One reason why Job's friends failed so miserably to comfort him was because they were 'strangers to suffering.' From the way they spoke to and about Job we can concluded that Eliphaz, Bildad, and Zophar had not suffered any significant loss and pain in their lives. There are so many friends who are strangers to suffering, and therefore do not know how to comfort a friend in pain and sorrow. Job's friends had never been the recipients of the comfort that a sufferer needs. One of the prerequisites for the ministry of comfort is to first become a recipient of comfort. Their lives of ease in the comfort zone disqualified them from being able to comfort their friend in need.

"Praise be to the God and Father of our Lord Jesus Christ, the Father of compassion and the God of all comfort, who comforts us in all our troubles, so that we can comfort those in any trouble with the comfort we ourselves have received from God." (2 Corinthians 1: 3-4)

Many friends have never received divine comfort through human discomfort. The only comfort we can give to another person is the comfort we ourselves have experienced at a time when we suffered. That was a key reason for their incapacity to comfort Job. They tried sympathy without empathy, but sympathy without empathy leads to apathy, and it was their apathy that caused them to mercilessly argue with a man who was fighting for every breath everyday to hang on to dear life. 'Participation in all man's sufferings qualifies him to be a comforter.' The question is: When you see your friend suffering will you be fit to comfort them?

A COMFORTING TONGUE:

"The Lord God has given me an instructed tongue; to know the word that sustains the weary." (Isaiah 50: 4)

The best learning that a friend can have experience of is to know how to comfort troubled consciences, and speak pertinently, properly and plainly in the various circumstances of your suffering friends. An ability to do this is a God given gift, and is one of the best gifts that every concerned friend should seek. Holding back kindness and comfort to suffering friends means forsaking the God who created and gave you life and all things.

How easy it is to look down on those less privileged and fail to appreciate the difficulties of others. When you see others suffering, do you catch yourself saying things like; "it is his own fault", "He got what he deserved?" or "He has no one to blame but himself?" The Lord Jesus was moved by compassion when He saw the multitudes of hungry and thirsty people. True friends should be sympathetic and sensitive to each other and those around them. We can be better friends, better comforters and better representatives of God, if we could remember our suffering friends and those around us.

CHAPTER 5

FRIENDSHIP AND RESPECT

"Be devoted to one another in brotherly love, in honour preferring one another." (Romans 12: 10)

The word 'respect' means a feeling of deep admiration for someone or something elicited by the abilities, qualities, or achievements. Friends are to show due respect in a relationship, and to strive by showing mutual kindness to enhance the quality of the friendship. If these qualities are to be obeyed in a friendship, it would put an end to envy, heartburning, dissatisfaction and jealousy. Respect for one another produces contentment, harmony, love and order in the friendship and prevents discord and bitterness. Furthermore and especially, it would promote order, peace and beauty in the church and general communities. Disrespect is an enemy of progress and has changed the spirit of our society, so much to say that we have become enemies of each other, for which there is no just cause. True respect is being able to take notice of the gifts, graces and performance of each other, and to value each other accordingly, it is to be ready to praise one another, and eagerly to hear another praised other than you. Disrespect in friendship means to regard or treat each other without respect or be rude to another in word and deed. Friends who disrespect one another spend more time apart on days when they are quarrelling. Insults, putdowns and teasing are all forms of disrespect. Disrespect can sound like; 'you are nothing without me.' No matter how it sounds, disrespect is hurtful and can damage self-esteem and long-lasting friendships. Disrespect is tearing your friend apart instead of building him or her up. Disrespect in friendship involves making decisions without reference to the other friend who will be affected by the decisions. Respect and open communication creates a successful friendship, or repairs one that is broken.

RESPECT PLAYS AN IMPORTANT ROLE: In friendship respect plays a variety of roles. In a practical sense, it includes taking your friend's feelings, needs, thoughts, ideas, wishes and preferences into consideration. We might also say that it means taking all of these seriously, giving them worth and value. It also includes acknowledging your friend, being truthful to them, and accepting their individuality and mode of expression. Respect plays an important role in survival. If we think of friends walking in the desert wilderness we can imagine the one not respected by any of their friends could be left behind to die. Such a person would not be considered to have worth, importance, or value to the group. There is a value to be respectful which money cannot buy. There are fewer conflicts when friends respect one another.

'This is a value we all need in this world. we should start going by value, not only in big issues like peace talks or in world problems, but we should start from all but important issues like learning to respect each other.'

THE GREATEST THING WE DESIRE: It is very hard for someone to give respect if they are not getting any from their surroundings. This is one of the reasons people don't respect others or cannot seem to accept there are others who act and think differently. Respect is the most important thing in any relationship. If we don't respect others and think we are better than them, we will reach our end very soon. Friends should see, speak, listen and think with respect. A lack of respect for each other, because we are different in several ways, is the root cause of most conflicts in friendship. However, while we expect our friends to respect us, which is the greatest thing we desire from others, valuing and respecting another is easier said than done. Respect is not gender, race or education specific. You may not agree with your friend's beliefs, or like the way they dress or speak, but these are not reasons enough to disrespect them. To gain respect from others one must have self-respect first. You can only give what you have. Disrespect and criticism lower the serotonin in the brain, leaving us open to self-doubt. Respect and other forms of positive feedback elevate the serotonin level in the brain. Mutual respect leads to self-assured conduct that benefits the friendship. Again, I ask, who is your friend?

FRIENDSHIP AND COURTESY:

"But in your hearts set apart Christ as Lord. Always be prepared to give the reason for the hope that you have.

But do this with gentleness and respect, keeping a clear conscience, so that those who speak maliciously against your good behavior in Christ may be ashamed of their slander" (1 Peter 15:16)

Courtesy means showing a polite behavior. To be polite is to show in action or word a considerate regard for others. This is how friends should treat each other and courtesy should be extended to all people. Poor friends should not to be despised; bad friends should be honored, not for their wickedness, but for any other qualities. Abraham, Jacob and the apostles never failed to give due honor to bad men.

ROYAL VIRTUE: Courtesy means to be friendly-minded. **Timothy Eaton** founder of Eaton's department store, one of the most important retails businesses in Canada's history; succeeded by using virtues of courtesy. Courtesy was a royal virtue to the ancient Greeks. Kings were expected to be friendly to their subjects. The Athenians considered it a virtue that should characterize every man. Emperor Julia, who was greatly influenced by Christianity, exalted courtesy to the highest level in government. He taught that politics and law were to be governed by courtesy. Being courteous means being nice to people by giving them a hand in times of need, and showing them respect as human beings. It is a basic secular and humanistic virtue. You don't need to be a Christian to be courteous. Anybody can be courteous and almost everybody is to some degree, it is also a virtue greatly needed in friendship.

The opposite of courtesy, is being discourteous which is showing rudeness and lack of consideration for others. Therefore, being overbearing and tyrannical, which fitted

'**Saul of Tarsus,**' against his fellow men. Courtesy is just common sense. If you talk to your friend with respect and kindness, they will listen with the same spirit. If you blast them with a critical spirit, you will most likely get the same in return. Courtesy is a better way than cleverness. It is putting yourself in the same boat with the people you try to befriend. If you can't be courteous to your friends, then who can you show courtesy for?

'Nothing will develop a spirit of true courtesy except a mind filled with goodness and justness.' **Writer unknown (anonymous)**

ALL DOORS FLY OPEN: Common courtesy, politeness and good manners make up moral excellence. According to William of Wykeham, former Bishop of Winchester, chancellor of England and founder of Winchester and New College, Oxford said; "Manner and courtesy makes friendship."

Politeness must know no classification; our rich and poor friends must alike share in justice. Exclusive spirits that avoid friends whose level in life is not as extravagant as them, cannot aspire to the high honour of wearing the name as a true friend. The truly polite friend acts from the highest and noblest idea of what is right. According to poet Laureate Alfred Tennyson "The greater a man is, the greater the courtesy."

A courteous friend respects the individuality of their friends, just as they wish their friends to respect them. They never boast of their achievements to underrate their friends. They prefer to act rather than to talk, to be hidden rather than be seen, and, above all, they are known by their deep sympathy and quick attention to little things that cause pleasure or pain to their friends. In giving their opinion(s) they don't dogmatize; they listen patiently and respectfully to their friends. Frankness and kindliness mark all dealings with their fellowman.

A fine courtesy is a blessing in itself. The good-mannered can do without riches, for they are welcome wherever they go. All doors fly open to them. And they enter without money or price. They are as welcome everywhere as the sunshine.
"Courtesy has won more victories than gunpowder."
Writer unknown (**Anonymous**)

FRIENDSHIP AND CHARACTER:

"I will be careful to lead a blameless life, when you come to me." (Psalms 10: 2)

A friend, in the choice of a principle to guide him in his conduct, family, official relations and among friends, should act wisely and prudently. David behaved himself wisely in all his ways. Character is power and influence; it makes friends and creates funds, it draws favor and support opening a sure and easy way to wealth, honour and happiness. Though a friend may have small wealth, yet has good and gracious character, he or she will always command influence among their friends. True character carries with it influence which always commands the general confidence and respect of all friends. A good character is, therefore, to be carefully maintained for the sake of all friendships.

A GOOD NAME EXCELS:

"A good name is more desirable than great riches; to be esteemed is better than silver or gold." (Proverbs 22: 1)

A good name conveys the idea of good reputation. There are three crowns:
i. The crown of the Torah. ii. The crown of the priesthood. iii. The crown of royalty.

However, the crown of a good name excels them all. Character supports a man in many circumstances and there are many friends that have no name, but the word of the friend of character will go farther than all his or her riches. 'Remember that your real wealth can be measured, not by what you have, but by what you are.' Character is constant riches. What a person does is the real test of what they are. Noble deeds always enrich friendship, but rough friends' and bad habits destroy close relationships. You cannot buy, beg or steal character. You can only get it by building and earning it when acting on and utilizing your own thoughts and actions. Friends of good character are generally friends of good reputation. Reputation is that which your friends believe you to be; character is what you really have, without character you have nothing and you are nothing, except material bone and flesh.

The word character is derived from the Greek word; charakter (character) which, was originally used as a mark embossed upon a coin. Reputation is what others think about us, but character is what God and angels know about us. Having a good character means to act in a manner that is seen to be honorable, courageous, compassionate and ethical. The result of character is being looked upon with respect, an ability to overcome the difficult and feeling good about you. Your character is based on the opinions you have for friends as well as your personal view. Friends will trust a friend who has a reputation for being honest, reliable and responsible. Dishonesty can easily tarnish that reputation for which your friends consider you trustworthy.

CHAPTER 6

TYPES OF FRIENDSHIP

People have friends that they don't always trust. Many also have empty friendships that have nothing good to offer them. At times people who have everything to give simply do not get good friends. I believe a friendship is a partnership, and it involves an interchange. Friendship is a relationship in which both individuals can enjoy time together, where there are no ego issues, open conversations and refreshing loyalty. A good friend always appreciates the good qualities in a friend, tries to improve negative ones and encourages an honest and open transparent relationship. A good friendship is a source of inspiration and motivation, where they can learn from each others' successes and mistakes. Here are types of classic friendships we should be aware of:

FRIEND OF MUTUAL NEED: Some friends meet specific metaphysical needs. Some people have gaps in their lives in which they need to either give or take to fulfill something personal. By giving, they justify a trait they value in themselves and would like to ascribe to. By taking, they are able to fill a need. Some friends are able to both give and take with one another, which creates a lasting friendship for as long as the relevant needs arise. When nothing is being personally fulfilled in the friendship, it can begin to break down. Friends in this group are few. They will be there to support you during the ups and downs of life. Sometimes, we can find these types of friendship between married women, mother and daughter, close sisters, sisters and brother- in-laws. These are friends we will grow old with as they are often family connected.

FRIENDS OF LEISURE: These friends have agreed to join in socially and keep one another company when they are having fun. They enjoy their external behaviors and appreciate their talents i.e. playing poker, sense of humor, tastes in movies and so on. These friendships do not usually include a level of deep attachment. This is a very informal group of friends, also called 'Buddies who meet informally to have leisure time together. This group often consists of college and high school students, singles, and maybe sports teams. These friends usually go to clubs, bars, happy hours, etc. There is not much intellectual or professional connection, because the people in this group still do not have the need to explore more serious matters of life, or might not feel the comfort to seek advice on any issues.

FUNCTIONAL FRIENDSHIP: These friendships are usually based on convenience. The friend could be a roommate who you get along with but would never know outside of the prevailing situation, or a friend who can help during an event, maybe someone with whom you trade. Whatever the scenario, you share a mutual agreement between yourselves. This is a group for professional networking. At the beginning of the relationship, much of the conversation hovers around topics of mutual interest in specific professions, and gradually takes a more personal turn. In these friendships, the expectation is to learn, exchange information, ideas, concepts, trade and grow professionally. A lot of these friendships are formed in professional organizations. Most of these relationships grow deeper when both individuals can provide professional expertise and insights. We come across these friends in work places also. Sometimes, they take the form of mentors, of people we could count on in future.

FRIENDS OF PAST EXPERIENCE(S): Sometimes a friendship is formed primarily because both friends have been through many experiences together. These friends know a great deal about their individual lives. They have many shared experiences, or they share so many emotional gifts together that they have either become comfortable or 'stuck' with each other. In this case ending the friendship would involve someone being hurt.

ROMANTIC FRIENDSHIP: In this situation, one or both friends see the other as a potential romantic partner. This can also apply to people who would never actually get into a relationship, but nonetheless harbor fantasies about it. These friendships can sometimes be very real and long-lasting. Since these people want to grow closer, they open up and become as close a friend as possible to keep the door opening more and more. They are usually on their way to either beginning an amoral relationship, or translating the relationship into a perpetual flirtation.

ONE-SIDED FRIENDSHIP: Is when one friend is being used by the other. This can be for money, services, career advantage, sex, information, tactical social stance, living space, etc. I would include in this situation when the need of another individual, such as loneliness, is deliberately being manipulated. These relationships are generally unhealthy unless the one being taken advantage of is perpetually oblivious.

PROFESSIONAL FRIENDSHIP: Is a friendship formed between someone in a position of authority, such as a manager or teacher, and a subordinate or a student. These are friendships in which a power relationship and the threat of 'unprofessional behavior' form a permanent and measured distance between both individuals. These bonds can be very intense and important to both parties, but they are necessarily limited by the boundaries they were created in.

INTELLECTUAL FRIENDSHIP: Is a friendship in which there is little by way of shared values or interests. Both parties find the other philosophically or intellectually interesting. It is also shared by any two people who are mutually fascinated by the other's knowledge and/or background. This group has a very curious and intellectual mindset. Those involved can talk about anything without being embarrassed. Friends in this group are very few. They usually understand situations logically without mixing feelings. Often this group of friends are considerate, mature, well-developed and members have their own fulfilled lives. Sometimes, these groups are so deep into their own pursuits and quests in life, they might not be able to offer the time, however, when they do, it is mutually fulfilling.

SELF-ACTUALIZED FRIENDS: Friends in this group are of a perfect combination and are very rare to find. These friends have an amazing appetite for intellectual conversation, and open to discuss life's experiences, take care of their own needs, voice less complaints about life generally and respect other's views on life. In addition to that, they love to invest time to grow emotionally, professionally, intellectually, socially, and spiritually and know how to laugh and enjoy life. They do not try to change others and appreciate and respect their differences. Probably, they will grow old as friends. The friends in this group volunteer to give us feedback and advice about different aspects of life, not only because they care about people, but because they also want positive things to happen in people's lives.

SCHOOL, COLLEGE OR UNIVERSIRY FRIEND: (Memory Revisiting) There are a lot of friends in this group. If they have not kept in touch, most of them are acquaintances at this stage. Most likely they have changed since last seeing each other. They will most likely meet at reunions, alumni events. Much of the conversation are nostalgic and about the 'good old days.'

FRIENDSHIP OF PLEASUR: The most basic form of friendship is pleasure friendship. Here, friends stick together simply because of the pleasure each brings to the other. Friendships of pleasure tend to be short lived and engage only the most basic capacities. For this reason, said Aristotle that, such friendships cannot provide long-term happiness, not least because the kind of things we take pleasure in can change easily, causing us to cast old friends to the wind once they cease to provide the pleasure they once did. This type of friendship is normally built between the young as passions and pleasure are a greatest influence in their lives, and are characterized by such feelings as passion between lovers, or the feeling of belonging among a like -minded group of friends. It differs from the friendship of utility (below) as those who seek utility friendships are looking for a business deal or long- term benefit, whereas, in the friendship of pleasure, one seeks something which is at that moment pleasurable to one.

UTILITY FRIENDSHIP: Utility is the quality or state of being useful or profitable to a valuable end; as the utility of manure fertilization upon land. Utility friendship is friendship, which is adapted to satisfy the desire or want of each other. Friendships based on utility dissolve when the friends no longer find utility in one another. These break-ups are made more complicated when people are misled into thinking they are loved for their character and not for certain incidental attributes. Aristotle described a friendship of utility as "shallow and easily dissolved." He viewed it as such, because this type of friendship is easily broken and based on something that is brought to the relationship by the other person. An example of this type of friendship evolves in a trading relationship. He argues that friendships of utility are often between people of complementary needs, in order to maximize this trade. A more realistic name for this type of friendship would be an 'acquaintance' and could be described as the relationship between a person and their mailman. They greet each other, discuss the weather and petty talk, but when it comes down to it, there is no real relationship between them. Aristotle believed this is exactly why this type of friendship is for the aged.

WEAK BOND FRIENDSHIP: This type of friendship is broken when, no matter how small, some part of the relationship changes and is no longer beneficial to one or both of the individuals concerned. For example, say a person visits the same hair salon every month. However, a new salon has opened for business and provides better service for a cheaper price. The friendship built between the hair dresser or barber and the person getting their haircut will likely dissolve, as it is cheaper to use the services of the cheaper salon. Because of this, the friendship of utility has a very weak bond between the individuals in the relationship and in this aspect; it is quite similar to the friendship of pleasure.

TELEPHONE FRIENDSHIP: This is when two people keep in regular contact by telephone. Naturally, this relationship or friendship has limitations, but there is something very helpful about the few minutes of conversation. One thing I have noticed is that it tends to be substantial. Telephone conversation is expensive, so when you realise the cost is increasing, you make sure the subject matter is important and beneficial. This friendship is not cheap relationship, but what keep it alive are expressions of appreciation, encouragement and inquiry after the other.

TREASURE FRIENDSHIP: We all need treasure friends. They are friends who have something to teach us because they are better at something or more knowledgeable about something that we need or want. These are friends who have got nothing to do with jealousy, competition, intimidation. What is more gracious and fortunate than knowing a friend who can teach you something? So let us ask, whom can we follow down the hill of life and learn from by example? Where is the friend who is not afraid to show us our need for improvement and how to make it happen?

BARRIER: A barrier is something that bars, keeps out or hinders progress. There are barriers in many friendships. Some men do not want to get close to another who appears superior to them. This attitude has to be broken if we are to grow and explore. In my world, I decided if there are men who would open their lives to me, I would be ready to benefit from all they had to offer. Today I delight in friends who have achieved more, who are godly, who are smarter, and whose lives seem to have a far greater character than mine. These friends are a treasure. Some call this type of friend a mentor. Mentoring is a highly specialized form of friendship. It is a great moment for an older and more experienced man who wants to pour himself into the young. The Lord Jesus Christ prepared His disciples for His leaving; His investment profited the whole world. Moses mentored and instructed Joshua. His investment paid off handsomely. It was quite a friendship.

"We have to have more than textbooks, we need text-people"
Abraham Joshua Heschel. (American Rabbi and Jewish Theologian 1907-72)

STAGES OF FRIENDSHIP:

"When I was a child, I talked like a child; I thought like a child, I reasoned like a child. When I became a man, I put childish ways behind me." (1 Corinthians 13: 11)

We should despise our childish attitudes in friendships when we are grown up to be adult men and women. The idea here is that our knowledge of who a friend is when we were children should vary from our idea of who is a friend when we reach adulthood. As we advance in years, we should lay aside childish feelings, views, ideas and plans concerning friendship, and pick up on more mature feelings, views, ideas and plans. So shall our friendships prosper?

WILLIAM RAWLINS: William Rawlins, a well-known communications scientist and Stocker Professor from the School of Communication Studies at Ohio University, studied thousands of friendships and set down a series of stages that a friendship usually goes through. His list is considered to be comprehensive. In the kindergarten your idea of a friend was the person who lent you the red crayon when all that was left was the black one. In the first grade your idea of a friend was the person who helped you to stand up to the class bully. In the second grade your idea of a good friend was the person who shared his or her lunch with you when you did not have any. In the third grade your idea of friend was the person who saved a seat on the bus for you. In the fourth grade your idea of a friend was the person who let you copy their homework when you had not done it. In the fifth grade your idea of a friend was the person went with you to a party so you wouldn't be alone. In the sixth grade your idea of a friend was the person who changed their schedule so you could have someone to sit with at lunch. In the seventh grade your idea of a friend was the person who gave you a ride in their car, and convinced and consoled you in your difficult times.

Now, your idea of a friend is still the person who gives you the better of the two choices; helps you fight off those who try to take advantage of you; thinks of you at times when you are not there; reminds you of what you have forgotten; helps you put the past behind you but understands when you need to hold on to it a little longer. This friend stays with you so that you have confidence, going out of their way to make time for you, helping you deal with pressure from others and smiles for you when you are sad, or even helps you become a better person.

Most importantly, this friend is one who loves you.

THE MATURE STAGE: The early stage of friendship is the beginning of a process of developing a true friendship. This is meeting a person for the first time during normal routine activities. This person at this stage is just an acquaintance. You have brief chats and get along well with them, but at this point know very few details about them. This particular individual is an acquaintance because you just met and wish to know them but still don't know enough about who they really are. However, in this stage there is a series of testing carried out by both sides. It is done to foresee whether this relationship can mature into friendship or you will remain just acquaintances.

The first step to take is disclosure of your personal information to them as a way of showing a level of trust and affirmation to be open to have a friendship. This information is usually telephone details, home address, work place and maybe your safe personal experiences. If they fail or insists to hold back their own similar information, then it is better to stop forcing them to be a friend and to remain as an acquaintance. Friendship is a two sided and willing process.

At this stage, the open-minded acquaintances can become fond of each other. There is giving and receiving of gifts. The acquaintance begins to make sacrifices for the sake of the other. They feel the urge to spend more time with each other. This kind of urge is inflamed by the common ground between them. This is the stage where being an acquaintance evolves into the early stages of being friends, therefore, getting to know each other mentally, spiritually and physically. There is ninety-five percent of knowing, respecting and understanding each other; the five percent is made up of total secrets that are unnecessary to reveal. They know when it is suitable to visit, surprise or give assistance. To reach this stage there must be self-disclosure. Reaching the mature stage means they will disclose their private life to and have it reciprocated, thereby turning an acquaintance into a friendship.

PENETRATION: As friendship develops, those involved penetrate deeper and deeper into their private and personal matters. This exposes vulnerabilities, so trust has to be developed along the way. Penetration goes through a number of stages.

1. Orientation stage: Here, we play safe with small talk and simple, harmless clichés.
2. Exploratory affective stage: We now start to reveal more of ourselves, expressing personal attitudes concerning moderate topics though we are not yet comfortable to lay ourselves bare. We are still feeling our way forward. This is the stage of casual friendship and many relationships do not go beyond this stage.
3. Affective stage: Now we start to talk more about private and personal matters. We may use personal idioms. Criticism and argument may arise. There may be intimate touching and hugging at this stage.
4. Stable stage: The friendship now reaches a plateau in which personal things are shared and each can predict the emotional reactions of the other person. In building a friendship, notice the stages and do not try to hurry things too much.

FRENEMY FRIENDS: meaning; a person with whom one is friendly despite a fundamental dislike or rivalry.

"Attend to me, and hear me; don't turn away from my plea! Listen to me and answer me; I am worn out by my worries. I am terrified by the threats of my enemies, crushed by oppression of the wicked. If it were an enemy that mocked me, I could endure it; if it were an opponent boasting over me, I could hide myself from him. But is it you, my companion, my acquaintance and close friend. We took sweet counsel with each other and worshipped together in the house of God." (Psalm 55: 12 - 14)

Ahithophel was to David a friend whom he acquainted with all his secret feelings, but he was an enemy. Ahithophel was a Frenemy. Frenemy (alternately spelled "frienemy) is a portmanteau of 'friend' and simultaneously, a competitor, rival or even an enemy. The term is used to describe a personal, geopolitical, and commercial relationship both among individuals and institutions. The concept of the Frenemy has been around for a long time. It is not difficult to find examples in literature of two people who genuinely like one another on one level, but are mortal enemies on another level. The source of the conflict may be love, lust, power, greed, or any other underlying motive that creates a situation where the two parties like each other and at the same time can't stand one another at another level.

WHERE TO FIND A FRENEMY: Frenemies can exist among social groups as well as in the workplace. For example, two neighbors or friends may participate in community activities and appear on the surface to get along very well. At the same time there is a competition between the two that may bubble to the surface for any reason at all. Perhaps both wish to be thought of as being the most attractive and hard working, or wish to be thought of as the most helpful neighbour or friend. The competition may become so intense that the two neighbours or friends begin to look for small ways to discredit one another in the eyes of the rest of their neighbours or friends. The process of Frenemy may also function in the reverse. That is, two parties may choose to present a public appearance of being opponents, while in fact enjoying a friendly relationship in private. Secret lovers or friends may in fact be Frenemies in this, or two individuals who are competitors in the business world may actually be weekend buddies. Frenemy is a term that is often used to refer to a business colleague that one maintains a friendly relationship with, but who is in fact an opponent. Within a business setting, a Frenemy may be a co-worker, who has a desire to secure your job by discrediting you, while presenting a friendly front at the same time. At the same time, an individual may become a Frenemy as means of keeping tabs on someone he or she thinks is out to get them.

SIBLINGS CAN BE FRENEMIES:

"One night Joseph had a dream, and when he told his brothers about it, they hated him even more. They saw him in the distance, and before he reached them, they plotted against him and decided to kill him." (Genesis 37: 3-30)

Joseph was hated by his siblings because his father loved him, which made them jealous and insecure. So is it common for those loved by God, neighbours, bosses, etc., to be hated by the people around them; when heaven blesses, hell curses. Joseph served them, but they made him their Frenemy.

I believe everyone has one or knows someone that has a Frenemy. Siblings are good examples of potential Frenemies, except you usually would not abandon your brother or sister like you can with a normal Frenemy. Rivalry and jealousy between sisters and brothers can often turn into a Frenemy scenario and behavior, which is not just restricted to children. I have known many siblings who have taken their intense rivalry with them throughout their lives and have gone on to be the best of Frenemies you could imagine. That is, they have a really close bond on one level but love getting one over on the other.

FRENEMIES CAN BE DANGEROUS:

"They said to one another, here comes that dreamer. Come on now, let us kill him and throw his body into one of the dry wells. We can say that a wild animal killed him. Then we will see what becomes of his dreams." (Genesis 37: 19-20)

Joseph's siblings could not imagine doing him homage, and this was what they plotted to prevent by having him murdered. Men that rage at God's plans are aiming to defeat themselves.

'God's providence often seems to contradict God's purpose, even then they are serving them, and working at a distance towards the accomplishment of them.'

Sometimes the Frenemy can be a dangerous person to have around and can turn from being the kind of friend you know is secretly envious, to the kind of friend who undermines you and turns your life into a living hell. I have known Frenemies to completely cross a line and start stealing from the other so-called friends. Money, spouse, clothes, jobs, other friends, are all targets of the Frenemy. They could spread rumours and lies and cause untold havoc, fights and arguments. Needless to say these Frenemies are everywhere, and this stands as a warning to everyone. There are friends out there who delight in seeing other friends suffer and who are so envious of someone, they will do their best to bring that person down. So you have been warned! Watch out for your Frenemies!

HOW TO DEAL WITH THE FRENEMY:

"But I call to the Lord God for help, and He will save me. Morning, noon, and night my complaints and groans go up to Him, and He will hear my voice." (Psalm 55: 16-17)

"Listen to me, you that know what is right, who have my word fixed in your hearts. Do not be afraid when people taunt and insult you; they will vanish like moth-eaten clothing! But the deliverance I bring will last forever; my victory will endure for all time." (Isaiah 51: 7-8)

David was driven from his home, his throne and from the house of God, forsaken by his Frenemy Absalom. But his faith did not fail, he trusted in God, and believed that God was able to deliver him.

Let not those who embrace the gospel faith be afraid of their Frenemies, who will do and say all manner of evil against you. Do not be disturbed by those opprobrious speeches, nor be made uneasy by them; as if they would be the ruin of their reputation and honour. Do not be afraid of their executing menaces, nor be deterred thereby from your duty, neither be frightened into any sinful companies, or driven to take indirect courses for your own safety. Let us not fear the reproach of our Frenemies, for they are nothing but human beings.

BE CAREFUL: Some Frenemies are hard to spot. After all, they are as manipulative as you can imagine. If a Frenemy has made it into your inner friendship circle, you must be careful, kicking this person out of your life or group might make matters worse. Should you decide that you would rather take a chance at losing a Frenemy from your life altogether, do it the right way. Phase them out. You can do this by enforcing a dwindling phone call, or when you talk to them make no plan to hang out soon. Leave the conversation closed, in essence don't ask questions or make statements that may require a follow-up. Put a halt on the secret exchanges. Don't give them ammunition! The list of ammunition includes things like: gossips, personal struggles, financial woe and pending decisions, as they can be dangerous with the right kind of information. So discern, as we should depend on the power, wisdom and knowledge of God to be able to deal wisely and prudently with the Frenemy.

SUPERFICIAL FEELINGS:

"But then they would flatter him with their mouths, lying to Him with their tongues; their hearts were not loyal to Him, they were not faithful to His covenant." (Psalm 78: 36-37)

Here are some characteristics of a superficial friend. Just as their friendship is superficial so are their feelings towards their friends. If they speak what is good, it is ordered more effectually to deceive. Their heart, the seat of feelings, is distinguished from the mouth, the organ of words. Superficial friends make a profession of friendship, but all is hollow and deceitful. They flatter with their tongue; their heart is full of all kinds of deception. I fear this is too true a picture of the human race. Obviously, it is better to have many friends, but there is a limit to how many intimate friendships one can sustain, and it is preferable to have a few close friendships than many superficial ones. While we need friends in our troubles and pains, friendship is more pleasant in prosperity.

POOR TREATMENT: The feelings we have for our friends should be the same as we have for ourselves. For instance, a good friend wishes good things for their friends, while enjoying their company, and shares their personal joys and sorrows. This can also be said of our relationship with ourselves, our own ego, even in the case of bad people, who treat both themselves and their friends poorly. Some people feel goodwill towards a friend in whom they perceive some merit or goodness, but this feeling is different from friendship or even affection, because it is superficial and not necessarily requited.

BENEFACTORS: A benefactor simply means a friendly helper. Benefactors seem to love those whom they have benefited more than the beneficiaries love in return. This love is like the love of an artist for their work, because the benefactor is to some extent responsible for making the beneficiary. It is also more pleasurable to do good actively than to receive good passively. Many friends have no friendly feelings towards their debtors, but only wish that they may be kept safe with the view to what is to be obtained from them. While those who have done a service to others feel friendship and love for those they have served, even if these are not of any use to them and never will be! This is true of craftsmen, as they love their own handiwork better. This is what the position of benefactors is like, for what they have treated well is their handiwork, therefore they love this more. Some benefactors are friends, who will only befriend you for what you have. Their aim is getting more than their fair share of advantages, and a friend wishing for self advantage criticizes their neighbour and stands in their way.

SELF-LOVE: Those who denigrate self-love are thinking of people who seek the greatest honors and pleasures only for themselves. A good friend who is self-loving will seek only what is best for themselves, which will be consistent with what is best for all. A good friend will do seemingly unselfish acts, such as taking risks for friends or giving away money, but will do these things because they are noble and are motivated by self-love. Many a time we think of self-love as a bad thing because we normally think of it in terms as being selfish. The person who selfishly seeks the benefit of utility will callously seek out wealth and honor, not caring who is crushed along the way. In the same way, the person who selfishly seeks the benefit of pleasure will callously seek out sex, good food and other pleasures, not caring who gets hurt along the way. These are both inferior forms of self-love; friends who seek only utility or pleasure for themselves are not treating themselves well, just as people who use friends for utility or pleasure rarely treat those friends well. It is best to love a friend for their good character, and that is also to love oneself. The person who seeks true personal goodness will aim at a virtuous life that consists not only of health and prosperity, but also one that is magnanimous and amiable. Self-sufficiency refers to the state of not requiring any outside aid, support, or interaction, for survival, it is therefore a type of personal autonomy. Epicurus advocates self-sufficient simply as a precondition for friendship. If a good person is self-sufficient, it follows that he or she has no need of friends. However, friendship is one of the greatest gifts in life, so in my opinion a good person cannot achieve perfect happiness without friends.

MALE FRIENDSHIP:

"After David had finished talking with Saul, Jonathan became one in spirit with David, and he loved him as himself. From that day Saul kept David with him and did not let him return to his father's house." (1 Samuel 18: 1- 4)

This is the bond of friendship Jonathan formed with David. Each found in the other the affection that they did not find in their own family. They loved each other with a pure fervent heart. No love was lost between them, each was worthy of the other. Friendships are an important part in a man's life. Friends are those men and/or women you can count on when you feel weak and low-spirited. They will back you up even when the whole world is against you. Friends are those that will cheer you up when you lose a job or go through difficult marital problems. While male friendship looks like a simple relationship, its history is actually quite interesting and complex. However, how men express those principles in a friendship has gone through great changes in the course of human history.

HISTORY OF MALE FRIENDSHIP: In times past, men viewed male friendship as the most fulfilling relationship a person could have. It was called **'The Heroic Friendship.'** Heroic friendship was between two men that were intense on an emotional and intellectual level. Examples of heroic friendship exist in many ancient texts from the Bible e.g. David and Jonathan. A male friendship that captures the essence of the heroic friendship is the relationship between Achilles and Patroclus, the Greek heroes who had a deep and extremely meaningful friendship. When Patroclus was killed Achilles was beside himself with grief for days. After the funeral, Achilles took to the battlefield to avenge the death of his best friend.

As we move through time, male friendship, during the 19th century, was marked by an intense bond and filled with deep feeling and sentimentality. A fervent bond did not necessarily imply a sexual relationship. Men during this time freely used endearing language with each other in daily interaction and letters. It was even common during this era for men to share a bed to save money. The great emancipator, Abraham Lincoln, shared a bed with a fellow named Joshua Speed for a number of years. Some scholars have concluded that this means Lincoln was gay. However, most scholars concluded that there was no homosexuality going on between them, they simply enjoyed a close and comfortable male friendship.

OVER AFFECTIONATE: There are several reasons why men were sometime so over affectionate with each other in the past. First, men were to have affectionate male relationships with each other without fear of being called a 'queer,' which was pleasingly odd, because the idea of homosexuality, as we know it today, did not exist then.

Affectionate feelings were not strictly labeled as sexual. There wasn't even a name for homosexuality; instead, it was referred to as 'the crime that cannot be spoken of.' Another reason for intense male friendships was that men and women basically lived separately until they got married. There wasn't much interaction between the sexes at that time. This separation led many young men to fulfill their needs for physical affection and emotional companionship with each other.

MEN WHO LIVE LONGER: Today, when a man is free to form a close intimate association with females, he generally does not feel the need to embrace his close buddy and express his love, except when they are maybe intoxicated. It is sad that our society prevents men from connecting with each other on a more emotional and physical level. I am not talking about crying and holding each other's head in our lap, and I can't say I long for those past days' of friendly bed-sharing. But men are often missing out on the benefits of close male friendship or bonding. Studies reveal that men who have several close friends are generally happier and live longer than men who don't.

QUALITIES OF MALE FRIENDSHIP: There are great differences between male and female friendship. Below are some admirable qualities of friendship between men:

1. **TRUE LOYALTY:** Many female friends will complain about one or more of their husband's friends. The disliked friend would usually be a guy the husband has known even longer. The woman will be bemused as to why her husband is still friends with this character when on the surface they no longer have much in common.

These women miss the nature of male friendship, which is all about loyalty.

2. **BEING STRAIGHTFORWARD:** When a man is bothered by something that his friend is doing, he usually tells. Them, then they discuss it, sometimes heatedly, and most times move on. A man generally does not keep burning angst bottled up inside, waiting to explode. And when men no longer get along, they most often simply go their separate ways without much fuss or ado. Not so for a lot of the female friendships I have seen. Many women, and sorry to say, some Christian women, are cruel to one another. They not only part ways, but often engage in emotional warfare designed to crush each others spirit. Men usually keep things more straightforward.

3. **STANDING BY:** It has been said that female friendship can be symbolized by two women standing face to face, while a male friendship can be symbolized as two men standing back to back, while looking outward. So here's to having a buddy, a brother to take on the world with. Long live male friendship.

FEMALE FRIENDSHIP:

"And she said, look, your sister-in-law is gone back to her people and her gods. Go back with her. But Ruth said, 'Don't urge me to leave you or to turn back from you. Where you go I will go, and where you stay I will stay. Your people will be my people and your God my God. Where you die I will die, and there I will be buried. May the LORD deal with me, be it ever so severely, if anything

but death separates you and me.' When Naomi realized that Ruth was determined to go with her, she stopped urging her. So the two women went on until they came to Bethlehem." (Ruth 1: 15-19)

Ruth makes a more perfect surrender, which has never been made of friendly feelings to a friend. "I will not leave you. I will follow you." This is an extraordinary attachment in a friendship. Her words expressed a love and loyalty that a friend could not reject, and such a determination that Naomi her friend and mother-in-law gave up urging her to return to Moab. Ruth's word implied a solemn vow, which may be paraphrased; "May a severe judgment befall me if I am not true to our friendship."

SHARING FEELINGS: Many couples refer to their spouses as best friends. But close friendships among women are very different. The result of a recent 'Harris Interactive survey,' has found that 64 percent of women choose to talk to female friends rather than spouses or mothers about their relationship and sex: **"My best friend is so important to me that I can barely quantify our relationship,"** Stella Mackay said of her pal Moira Callianan Little. MacKay said;

"I know any advice she gives me is out of pure love for me. I don't know anyone else who I could be so honest with without fear of the relationship being damaged. Between us, there is no fear at all."

The depth of emotion and lack of fear are the essence that makes female friendship different from that of men. Male friendship is more based on common interest or skills, while females' are based on the sharing of feelings. Women are far more likely than men to join formal or informal support groups to help one another deal with issues. They are given permission to rely on one another and seek support from one another. Men socialize for self-support. Female friendships can be more volatile than males' because they are in a way more intense. In general, females may expect more time and emotional attention from their female friends than men do from their male friends. Women also, are more likely to carry a mess and bear a grudge.

"We just seem to need our friends more than men do." Sarah Sentilles: Scholar and author.

"And Mary got up and went into the hill town with haste, into a city of Judah; and entered into the house of Zachariah and greeted Elisabeth. When Elizabeth heard Mary's greeting, the baby leaped in her womb, and Elizabeth was filled with the Holy Spirit. She cried in a loud voice and said, 'blessed are you among women, and blessed is the fruit of your womb."
(Luke 1: 39-43)

Here is the picture of two women, friends and cousins, expressing their joy. Mary visited Elizabeth not as a common friend making a visit, but as a lover. Mary was not afraid to tell Elizabeth all about her situation. Elizabeth was the wife of a priest and ahead of her in years, yet she was not peeved that her younger cousin and friend, who were in every way inferior, should have the honor of being the mother of the Messiah. But she rejoiced with her, a good friend should by no means feel bad that their friends are more highly favored than them. Female friendship is different from males in many respects. Men don't probe into each other's emotions and take things easy during crisis situations. Here is where women score higher. Elizabeth probed into the life of her cousin and friend Mary. Women know how to comfort and what words to use to make sure that their friend feels aright. Elizabeth comforted Mary in her confused state.

"In a loud voice she said; 'blessed are you among women, and blessed is the fruit of your womb.'"

HISTORY OF FEMALE FRIENDSHIP: In the past, only men enjoyed this thing called friendship. They claimed that women had inferior status, and that prevented them from enjoying such deep relationships. Even the great philosophers, Plato and Aristotle, never accepted the possibility that women could also be friends. However, during our times, places like schools, salons and markets became more and more popular. It was in these places that women finally began to really come into contact with each other and to spend quality time together.

KATHERINE PHILIPS (Anglo Welsh poet 1632-1664):
A young Katherine Foley went to boarding school in her formative years. It was in this environment that she began to cherish her interaction with the other women around her. There, away from the prejudiced judgments of men, she began writing poetry about those new-found friendships. Her connections with other women became particularly important when she married Colonel James Philips, a man almost forty years older that her. Soon after, she formed the society of friendship in which she and a small group of women wrote poems of love and friendship to one another. Each member took on a nickname, Philips became known from that point on as Orinda. She began writing to her friends. Ladies, forming this kind of group, would be a great way to expand their friendships. In reading Katherine

Philips works, you will see images of sighs, tears, and breathe to imply friendship. She suggests a connection between the mind and soul of two friends, is a connection that is not easily broken. Katherine Philips will always serve as a reminder that true female friendship is an Eden on earth.

DELARIVIER MANLEY (English author, playwright and political pamphleteer 1663-1724) Although female relationships and their influence may have been previously hidden, Delarivier Manley exposed the power that female friendship can have on society. Manley explored female relationship and how women have used them to influence society. She focused on relationships between noblewomen and servants, and how these sexualized relationships are viewed in the social and political sphere. She exposed the relationship between Queen Anne and one of her advisors, Sarah Churchill. Manley's immensely popular attack on Churchill's intimacy and powerful influence with the queen were perceived as emblematic of an indecorous appropriation of political power practiced by those aristocratic ladies. The satire of Queen Anne and Sarah Churchill demonstrates to women how powerful female friendship can be. She also showed how quickly public opinion can turn against those suspected of sexual impropriety.

ELIZA HAYWOOD (English Writer, actress and publisher 1693-1756) For those of you middle class women that are looking for entertainment and a break from everyday life, Eliza Haywood is the author for you. Haywood is a writer who addressed the very theme in the female spectator was social contact. Female community and opportunity outside the domestic sphere are some of the most important issues facing women today. In her series of discussions, she investigated in her longer fiction the problem of female opportunity and limitation. More specifically, she concerned herself with how women might operate effectively within the social restriction that envelops them. What does this mean to you? Haywood realised most of the women will not run away and leave their husbands, children and responsibilities in search of adventure and female friendship. Therefore, women should seek or be provided with information, entertainment, and didactic advice, that can consume them in the privacy of their own homes.

IMPORTANCE OF FEMALE FRIENDSHIP: The creation of friendships among women is of vital importance to their well-being and survival. Friendships allow men and now women, the opportunity to partake in relationships based on choice instead of kinship. Women face subordination in many aspects of their lives, but by making friends they assert their autonomy over who they choose to spend time with. You see how men move away from their kinship ties and towards more friendships and what do they achieve in doing so, great power! Women can make that a reality for themselves as well. Some of the women are single, but many others are married. Friendship may not be able to correct the problems in your marriage, but can promise you another place to turn in times of hardship. True friends will always be there for you. They will offer advice, a shoulder to cry on, or simply a listening ear. Remember, because women choose their friends they remain dedicated to them. And friends are 'one soul in two bodies' as Aristotle has noted.

Although, it's true to say friendship among women is more social than political. These new relationships are forums where you can find true companionship. The network of female friends will support you intellectually, spiritually, and socially. Female friendship can promote your own excellence and own space for culture. Women love to have their own little corner of the world, where the things they think and feel matter.

MOTHER AND DAUGHTER FRIENDSHIP: A landmark UCLA (University of California, Los Angeles) study suggests that friendships between women are special. They shape who you are presently and who you will be in future. Female friendship soothes any disorder in their inner world, fills the emotional gaps in their marriages, and helps them remember who they really are. A woman needs an emotional bond. An expert has said that, in friendship, women look for identity and emotional support. So in life, it's important for women to have close friendship with other women. Physiologically, as mentioned before, females have a greater need to emotionally bond with other. Whereas, many men get by with loose, casual relationships with other men, but women tend to look for nurturing and more emotionally fulfilling bonds with other women. This need starts in childhood and increases during adolescence, when teenage girls find support from their female peers. Often, less emphasis is placed on the mother- daughter bond as teens venture out and test the waters of young adulthood. But once attaining full adulthood, many young women re-establish the mother-daughter bond as one of their primary female friendships.

GET EDUCATED: Women, you might be asking yourselves, why would female friendship matter to me? Why would I concern myself with such matters, when I am happily married and have a loving husband and have a loving family? Although your domestic life may seem safe and secure, the society we live in can be a very hostile place. Since women are at times seen as the inferior specie, your only resource is to trust God and build alliances with women like yourself. In order to understand the importance of these feminine relationships, you need to first understand the position you find yourself in as a woman, whether that is as a Christian or an unbeliever.

Here are some facts about the social, legal and marital status. Divine and natural laws view women in two different states: married (feme covert) and single (feme sole). A single woman is allowed more social freedom than a married woman. She can go out to parties, funerals, to Church, travel anywhere at anytime, visit and be visited by friends at anytime without permission from any man. She may wear whatever she chooses, spend money however she desires, have as many friends as she wants. But, once she gets married, she loses many of these so-called liberties. As a wife, you will no longer be seen as individual but instead you merge into one with your husband. The word of God commands wives to:

"Submit to your husband as to the Lord." (Ephesians 5: 22)

Women should understand the changes in life, and how they can use these changes to the best of their advantage.

CHALLENGES TO FEMALE FRIENDSHIP: It is necessary to point out some of the challenges of female friendship. Much of our society does not fully accept or celebrate friendship among women. Because you are women you face different challenges socially, your friendship cannot simply join the realm of friendship among men. Therefore, some people will pass various judgments on you if you choose to forge ahead in your friendship with other women. There is a school of thought that believes that because you choose to be friends with women, you are somehow rejecting all men. They fear that once you understand the benefits of female friendship, you will decide not to marry, and create a great splash in society. While that may be the case of some women, and we respect them for that choice, it is not a trend among all women, so there should be no cause for alarm. As mentioned above, some female friendships are forms of **'sapphism'** (lesbianism). This does not mean that all friendships are on this level, and should not be a cause for alarm if you are not a **'sapphist'** (Lesbian). But ladies, you should beware that there is a rise in diseases and arrests and prosecutions for crimes related to lesbianism, such as fraudulent marriages, public immorality, and even sodomy.

CONDITIONS OF FEMALE FRIENDSHIP: I would like to give three specific conditions whereby female friendship could be strengthened. The conditions are that a woman must be thoughtful, and passionate, and she must also have happiness, in order to achieve a successful and lasting friendship with herself and others.

"Thinking is a necessary condition of women friendship," **(Janice Raymond-***Feminist***)**

THINKING: The thinking I advocate is better described as thoughtfulness. Thoughtfulness is characterized, on the one hand, by the ability to reason and, on the other, by consideration and care. Women are raised specifically to think and care about others. This is more directly related to men and children, but can also mean caring for other women. Women do not have much choice, society describes that they give to and care for others. Where then is the time for a woman to think about herself? That is where thinking and thoughtfulness come together. For female friendships to be sustainable, a woman must be able to think of as well as be caring, considerate, and respectful towards other women. A woman's best friend is herself. If a woman does not know herself, it may be hard for her to sustain or create a friendship with another woman. The only way for a woman to lose a friendship with herself is to stop thinking. When a woman finds friendship with herself, she can no longer be lonely. Any conversation made with oneself may also be made with another person.

PASSION: Passion simply means overpowering emotion or any kind of feeling, by which the mind is powerfully affected. A passionate friendship upholds the integrity between thought and passion. In passionate friendship, there is no separation between the persons involved. Passion is part of what makes a woman an individual. In a thoughtfully passionate friendship, two women become their own person. It is important for a woman not to lose herself in the attachment to another woman. Passion is associated with relationships between lovers, more than relations between friends.

HAPPINESS: Happiness is associated with a person's moral purpose, found in the achievement of a purpose or a life's goal. If so, then a person or a woman can find happiness by finding her life's purpose. According to feminist Janice Raymond; *"Happiness is striving for the full use of one's powers."* It is attained by fulfilling certain ends or purposes. A woman should continually work towards and strive for happiness. It is not something that will find a woman on its own, she must seek it out. Female friendship gives women the ability to be 'life-glad'. It makes happiness a reality and provides the encouragement and environment for the full use of one's capacity to make friends. Friendship is a great thing that anyone can have, and when it is strengthened, it will benefit each person involved.

CAREFULNESS IN FEMALE FRIENDSHIP: Women must be careful to protect themselves from negative assumptions, especially since much of the correspondence and interaction of their friendship will focus on the feeling of passionate love and longing for each other. There are ways to avoid claims of lesbianism within female friendships that seem to work quite well. Protecting a façade of great conversation and classism will suggest that, because you are a true gentlewoman, there cannot be any cause to believe you are a lesbian. But don't forget that some of the most respected ladies are also the greatest lesbians! How do you avoid lesbianism? In your letters to your friends avoid using expressions like kisses and caresses or discussions of your friendly and loving gazes at one another, will be safe communication. Most of all, remember that the key to protecting friendship is to describe it as a sisterhood. This familiar reference suggests a nonsexual relationship and is a safeguard against narrow-minded opinions.

LOVE AND ACCEPT ALL IN FEMALE FRIENDSHIP: There are also a few important warnings regarding your place within the realm of friendship. Many friendships exist only among women of the same class. Most ladies would never dare to suggest interaction with the ruffians of society. I believe that as human beings we should respect all other human beings. Part of the reason for this distrust of the lower classes, is the fear in your unstable society of sexual transgression. As the middle class rises closer and closer to the upper classes, there is a sense of instability. Any bad habit, particularly, a sexual transgression, will threaten your social status. So, love and accept the lower classes in every way. Educate and pray for them, donate money to help them, but do not allow them into your circle of friends or you may endanger your newly-gained status and connection in the society.

BENEFITS OF FEMALE FRIENDSHIP: If we accept that the absence of a strong emotional connection results in extramarital affairs, it is logical to examine the female and male relations in their separate ways. Female friendship is a very interesting phenomenon. From the psychological point of view, this type of relationship contains elements, which are typically absent in male friendship. Female friendships resemble relations between mother and daughter, with the exception of one essential element, being the authoritative attitude of the mother towards the daughter. One of the women may dominate the friendship; however, she will rarely adopt the authoritative style of the mother.

Godly female friendships produce tenderness, warmth, support, empathy, and pleasant company which are able to neutralize the negative impact of family problems. Another essential element of the female friendship is the talk about their men. They are free to complain and express dissatisfaction without feeling guilty. Female friendship produces understanding and active support. At the same time, talking about men has positive effects on the women's intimate relationships. They may fantasize about men without actually cheating. But, remember what Jesus said in the famous Sermon on the Mount, which of course applies to both genders:

"You have heard that it was said, ' Do not commit adultery.' But I tell you that anyone who looks at a Woman lustfully has already committed adultery with her in his heart. (Matthew 5: 27)

Female friends can boost each other's self-worth through compliments, honest opinions, andsuggestions. In times of trouble, females seek one another out to ensure that their feelings are normal and healthy. From these interactions, female friends achieve an increased sense of happiness and fulfillment. Physical gains can be both internal and external. With happiness and validation comes a lowering of the heart rate, blood pressure, stress, and the tendency to have a better appetite, and the immune system and digestion work more efficiently.

POSITIVE EMOTIONAL BONDING: Here are some situations that can give women positive emotional bonding:

1. **Family ties:** Mothers, daughters, sisters, aunts, and cousins can form tight female bonds. These are often primary relationships in women's lives.

2. **Childhood/school friendship:** These relationships can end up being some of the longest-lasting female bonds in a woman's life.

3. **Mummy groups/others mothers:** such friendships arise out of a common need to support and be supported as a mother.

4. **Women with common interests:** Joining activities such as women's moments, cooking classes, trade unions, and volunteer organizations can promote friendship out of common goals and the nurturing of these goals.

5. **Co-workers (colleagues):** Other female colleagues, depending on the type of industry, can be supported in career goals and in the understanding of office tension.

CHILDHOOD FRIENDSHIP:

"And the city streets will be filled with boys and girls playing there." (Zachariah 8: 5)

To be healthy, children must engage in physical and intellectual activity. Children who are able to make friends and play are healthy, strong and active; they do not lie sick in bed or sit pining in the corner, but are always be hearty and cheerful, and able to play in the street. Parent should not begrudge children playing with their peers, it is their pleasant playing age, and it will do them much good and not harm them, but more build their communication skills and grow confidence. *(See: Lamentations 2: 11-12)* A child needs honest and modest recreations with his peers or friends to help him grow mentally, emotionally, physically and spiritually. *(See: Matthew 1: 16-17)*

CHILDHOOD'S TOUGHEST LESSON: One lesson learnt in childhood is how to be a good friend. Parents need to understand the emotional steps children take in building friendships. Every child is different, but, there does seem to be a process that children follow in learning how to make friends. Between the ages of 3 and 7, your child thinks of 'friends', as those with whom they play with most of the time. Somewhere between ages 4 and 9, children become gradually aware that other people might think differently than they do. Then a friend becomes someone who does things that please me. It is not until ages 6 through to 12 that kids begin to understand the reciprocal nature of friendship. The lessons of child friendship include learning how to discuss a problem, handle differences in opinion and find ways to compromise. Your child can learn those things without an adult's intervention. By dealing with other children and comparing their own behavior to others, they will build a stronger concept of self. Parents, please relax! Your children can and will work things out. It is not always easy. But it is a natural process that may not be successful immediately. There will often be mishaps throughout this period of discovery, but bad experiences are always part of learning a lesson in life.

BOYHOOD FRIENDSHIP:

"Among these were some from Judah: Daniel, Hananiah, Mishael and Azariah. The chief official gave them new names; to Daniel, the name Belteshazzar; to Hananiah, Shadrach; to Mishael, Meshach and to Azariah, Abednego." (Daniel 1: 6)

Daniel and his three friends were among the young men carried to Babylon. They stood together in all their endeavour and trials of life. The command of the king that they should be fed with the food and wine from his own table was to Daniel and his friends a test of their fidelity to the Lord and His law. Here is a picture of a determined boyhood friendship. They were honored for their unbroken purpose.

CONNECTION AND BELONGING: Boys, like girls, crave connection and belonging. Like all of us, boys need friends and suffer when they don't believe they have any, agonizing over the ups and downs of relationships. Many adults believe that, somehow, boys need friends less than girls do, though no boy is an island. Boys value their friends throughout childhood and adolescence and are happier and healthier when they have solid relationship with their peers.

Despite the common belief that girls are better in relationships, most boys consider their friends a vital part of their lives. Boys may actually be better at maintaining friendships than girls. A recent study of ten -to-fifteen-year-old boys and girls found that girl's friendship is actually more fragile. Girls tend to say and do hurtful things to each other more frequently than boys. Boy friendships are usually built around active play. Boys are a living definition of the phrase 'peer group.' They love games with rules, competition, and doing things together. Boys' play usually includes teasing, which can sometimes veer off into meanness, especially if they perceive another boy as weak or clumsy. Boys seem to enjoy, even need the opportunity to test themselves against others, and many lasting friendships begin with games and competition. Competence and skill are widely respected; being picked last for a team or left out altogether is an experience that can haunt a boy for years. Below is a great example of what boyhood friendship can lead to.

HARLEY DAVIDSON: One of the most powerful, reliable and expensive motorcycles, 'Harley Davidson,' was manufactured by the families of boyhood friends Bill Harley and Arthur Walter Davidson. The history of the Harley-Davidson motorcycle began in Milwaukee in 1903.

In Milwaukee, Bill Harley and Arthur Walter Davidson developed a one-cylinder motorcycle. It was a reliable and beautiful cycle which someone first bought in 1905; they then made 11 more motorcycles and then 154 in 1908. They went on to begin a company in a little wooden barn that was built by Davidson's father. The small company grew fast and another member of the Davidson family, William, joined them. In no time they hired about 20 employees in an especially build stone-factory. 1910 brought the legendary 'bar and shield' logo that was placed on the motorcycle. This became the defining symbol of Harley- Davidson to this day. The year 1912 saw a further growth of the Harley-Davidson company. Construction began on a new six- story factory. This is great motivational message to parents to allow and support their children to keep friends, not just friends but good and productive friends. You never know what may come out of it.

GIRLHOOD FRIENDSHIP: The Bible talks about so many powerful girls who had exploits in their time. This is to illustrate the power of girlhood friendship to support each girl as they grow into women. Girls have always formed strong bonds, especially in tough times. According to new research findings, having high performing same-sex friends is beneficial to girls to whom such friendship can promote academic success in high school. However, the same effect does not hold true for boys. Girls are agents in the process of educational attainment, not just by making their own choices, but also by influencing their friends to do same.

WHAT PARENTS SHOULD KNOW AND UNDERSTAND: In elementary school, many girls feel it's essential to have best friends. Best friends become a sort of currency, said Professor in Anthropology, Lawrence Cohen. The words, I will be your best friend' also mean, I have power over you' because I could take my friendship away. Relational aggression is the use of friendship as a weapon. Girls can gain power by forming close friendships that exclude other girls, although the act of forming a close friendship is not by nature exclusive. But it is what they do within those friendships and with those that can become aggressive due to gossiping, reneging on secrets or, even just by giving dirty looks to girls not considered cool. A lot of times girls bully each other because they feel jealous. Some girls are shy and do need help asserting themselves and getting to know other girls. Socializing with peers is sometimes best achieved informally. If your daughter has some friends and is liked by peers, she might need some encouragement and help to maintain the friendship. One of the best things parents can do for their girls is to encourage them to speak out their thoughts and feelings, and to help them stay connected to reality in the face of what a girl should look, act, and be like.

PEER PRESSURE:

"If your own brother, or your son or daughter, or the wife you love, or your closest friend secretly entices you, saying 'Let us go and worship other gods' (gods that neither you nor your fathers have known, gods of the people around you, whether near or far, from one end of the land to the other), do not consent or yield or listen to him. Show no pity nor spare him or conceal him." (Deutronomy 13: 6-8)

Here is a caution against the temptation or pressure from your nearest blood-relation and/or friends.

It is a call to prevent any seductive persuasion from our loved ones. It is the policy of the tempter to send his agents by the hand of those whom we love, whom we least suspect of any wicked plan against us. The enticement here is supposed to come from a brother, a sister, child, wife, friends and/or peers that are close. Satan tempted Adam and Eve and even tried to tempt our Lord Jesus Christ. We are therefore, warned to guard against a bad proposal when any person that tries it and pretend to have an interest in us, so that we do not sin against God, our family and ourselves in compliment to the best friend or peers we have in the world.

WHAT IS PEER PRESSURE: Making decisions on your own is hard enough, but when people get involved and try to pressure you one way or another, it can be even harder. People, who are your age like your classmate, are called peers. When they try to influence how you act, and try to get you to do something, it's called peer pressure. It's something everyone has to deal with, including adults. Peers influence your life, even if you don't realise it, just by spending time with you. You learn from them, and they from you. Peer pressure is a social influence exerted by another on an individual. The pressure is acted out by a peer group against others, often in an 'everybody is doing it' scenario. The end result of successful peer pressure is a changed behavior. Peer pressure can be both negative and positive.

NEGATIVE PEER PRESSURE: A definition of peer pressure would be an invitation to trouble by someone close to neither the child's nor the adults' age. Negative peer pressure actually begins when children are as young as two years old. Research shows that 87% of teenagers face a negative peer pressure situation daily. Negative peer pressure can be a dangerous tool against children's friendships, especially younger or insecure children. Children may be coerced into changing their behavior for the worse. Their friends may talk them into actions they may otherwise not have considered, like smoking, drinking of alcohol, stealing, fighting, cheating, skipping classes, lying, vandalizing, gossiping, staying out late, and driving too fast also sexual behavior. It is simply being forced into a certain way of living; because that is how everyone else you know behaves and so on. In the same vein, peer pressure has the same issues and is a common problem for adult friendships. They may be pressured in the same way as children, for example to go on strike, changing friends, buying an expensive appliance, and even into be unfaithful to their spouses. Peer pressure, is a social pressure and dominates pre-life. Many teens are becoming absorbed into different cliques, groups, and spending less time with their families and home work. Much of the personality of a teen can be shaped by a peer group, and a 'everybody else is doing it' attitude.

Positive peer pressure: Merriam Webster's dictionary states that a peer is; 'one of equal standing with another,' or 'one belonging to the same societal group that is based on age, grade or status.' When parents hear the words 'peer pressures' their faces usually take on a worried expression. When most people say this they are talking about this as a negative pressure. There is another side of this issue, though it is positive. Many people do not realize that peer pressure can have a positive effect on children; but kids have the opportunity to be a positive influence in the lives of other children by encouraging them to do good things.

A healthy part of every child's development is involvement with their peers. This is especially true during adolescences as teenagers develop a sense of independence from their parents.

Whenever significant numbers of peers interact formally or informally, they constitute a force to reckon with. When they share mutual respect, they will listen to, learn from, and secretly support one another in ways that can shape opinions, create resistance, or generate energy.

CLASSROOM PEERS: The potential role that children's classroom peer relations play in their schooling was investigated during for the first two months of kindergarten and the remainder of the school year. Measures of one hundred and twenty-five children's classroom peer relationships were obtained over three periods: i) on school entrance. ii) Two months later. iii) At the end of the school year. Measures of school experience, including children's school knowledge; anxiety, avoidance, and performance were obtained during the second and third assessment occasions. After controlling mental age, gender, and preschool experience, measures of children's classroom peer relationship were used to calculate their later school standard. Results indicated that children with a large number of classroom friends during school entrance developed more favorable school knowledge by the second month, and those who maintained these relationship liked school better as the year progressed. Making new friends in the classroom was associated with gains in school performance, and early peer rejection led to less favorable school performances.

ADULT PEER PRESSURE:

"You shall not raise a false report: put not your hand with the wicked to be unrighteous witness. You shall not follow a multitude to do evil; neither shall you speak in a cause to decline after many to wrest judgment. Neither shall you countenance a poor man in his cause." (Exodus 23: 1-3)

Here is a caution against being misled into evil by the influence of prevailing peers. It is a warning against departing or deviating from the straight path of rectitude by friends. We must enquire what we should do, not what our pressuring peers do, because we must be judged by our Lord and Master Jesus Christ, not by our friends or peers. We often think of peer-pressure as being the exclusive domain of our teenage sons and daughters. Perhaps our teens also think this way. In reality, this is not the case. Most adults who are working or studying would likely agree they frequently experience peer-pressure. In some respect, peer-pressure can be worse for adults than it is for young people. On the job, in the community or society etc, as most of us have peers that we enjoy, respect and cultivate. We also have peers that we abhor, ignore and avoid.

"And the king was sorry: nevertheless for the oath's sake, and those which sat with him to eat, he commanded it to be given her. And sent and beheaded John in the prison." (Matthew 14: 8-11)

Another reason why Herod murdered 'John the Baptist' was because of peer pressure, in fear that his peers would consider him a coward and would laugh at him. Those companions or peers may be unprincipled condemners of the word of God and man, yet the duelist against his own conscience, against the word of God, and seeks by deadly aim to murder another merely to gratify their dissolute friends. Pilate sentenced the Lord Jesus Christ, because of pressure from the people. (See: Luke 23: 23- 24)

It should be added, this is the cause of all adult guilt. Some adults are led along by others. They have not adequate enough resolve to follow the word of God. They are afraid of being called mean and cowardly by their wicked friends, and often sink low in vice and crime, never to rise again.

RESISTING PEER PRESSURE:

"My sons, if sinners tempt you don't give in." (Proverbs 1: 10)

Do not go where evil people go. Do not follow the example of the wicked. Don't do it! Keep away from evil! Refuse it and go on your way. Wicked people cannot sleep unless they have done something wrong. They lie awake unless they have hurt someone. Wickedness and violence are like food and drink to them. The road the righteous travel is like sunrise, getting brighter and brighter until daylight has come." (Proverbs 4:14-18).

The first big danger which besets friendship, in both young and old, is negative peer pressure. Those who have been spiritually and physically educated and trained to know and understand the correct way to go forward should never change direction. Not even the devil himself can lead a man into sin or wrongdoing until he agrees with him. The only safety is to be found in the power of saying a firm "No" to all the invitations to do wrong through your friends. This is the advice of wisdom.

How can you say no to bad advice from friends? Be firm as you stand true to God, stand true to yourself, your family, society and true to your nation and refuse to compromise. We should stand true to the Lord, whether; others honour, despise, criticize or condemn us. A care to keep ourselves free from peer pressure is necessary in order to gain acceptance with God and man. Don't allow you to be pressured the one ways or others, be honest and think for yourself.

MATURE ADULT FRIENDSHIP:

"The gray-haired and the aged are on our side, men even older than your father." (Job 15: 10)

Job and his friends were aged men. Job admitted that with the aged was wisdom, and in the length of days came understanding. Eliphaz here urges that on this principle he and his friend had a claim to be heard. This is a picture of older adult friendship.
John Wesley preached every day at the age of 88. Benjamin Franklin went to France in the service of his country aged 78, and wrote his autobiography after his 80th year. Pope Leo XIII inaugurated most of his enlightened policies after he attained the age of 70. Sophocles wrote his Oedipus at 90 years of age. Titian painted his masterpiece, the bronze doors of the sacristy of St. Mark, at aged 85. Fate is kind to a man who surrounds himself with good friends. These above mentioned people all had one thing In common, they were people who loved and made friends and thus lived long and achieved their goals.

CIRCLE OF FRIENDS: Many studies have shown the benefits of friendship on a positive social, emotional, and physical well-being. Having a strong circle of friends can be a good source for aging hearts and help the body's autoimmune system resist disease. People who have one or more good friends have better health than those who have only causal friends or no friends at all.

Friends are as important as families. In our society, many people turn first to their friends when they encounter crises because of distance from their families. People without friends are likely to feel isolated and lonely. In the world today, one out of three women and one out of every seven men aged 65 or older live alone. They need to reach out to friends for companionship, friendship, support, and human contact. In addition, men usually have a harder time dealing with being widowed than women. About two-thirds of older men reported they did not have a close friend, while 16% of widows reported having no friends.

Because of physical changes, loss, and retirement, friendship is very important for older people. Although casual friendship can help, one close friend can help relieve stress and depression. Friendship not only gives emotional support, but is also a way of helping, sharing, caring, and informing each other. Friendship can help enrich a person's physical emotional and social health and adjust changes through the challenging times of life.

IF YOU DON'T HAVE A FRIEND: If you don't have a friend, take the initiative to be a friend to someone else. For instance, join civic groups, volunteer organizations, community events, church activities, etc. These are good places to meet people and build a good relationship. When you attend a group meeting, have something to say. Be informed by reading the news, magazines, and books and find opportunities to speak to other people without waiting for them to do so. It is also very important to listen to what the person is saying to you. Remember, if you want to have a friend, you must be a friend. Above all, remember that the Lord Jesus Christ is your greatest friend, accept Him into your heart and you will be happy here and hereafter. Do you have a friend? If so, who is your friend?

FRIENDSHIP BETWEEN CROSS GENDER:

"After this, Jesus travelled about from one town and village to another, proclaiming the good news of the kingdom of God. The twelve were with him, and also some women who had been cured of evil spirits and diseases: Mary called Magdalene from whom seven demons had come out; Joanna the wife of Chuza, the manager of Herod's household; Susanna; and many others. These women were helping to support from their own means." (Luke 8: 1-3)

The Bible does provide examples of men and women working together to promote the cause of the kingdom. Paul lived and worked with Aquila and his wife Priscilla, he commended Phoebe to the Church in Rome, and implored Euodia and Syntyche, who were members of the Church, and women who labored with him, to be reconciled. Moreover, there was a group of women who apparently travelled with the Lord Jesus and His disciples, supporting His ministry out of their own resources. However, none of these examples tell us that men and women should develop and maintain friendship with the opposite sex outside the relationship of marriage. Certainly, the biblical men and women cited above were on friendly terms with one another. But cordiality is not the same as friendship.

HISTORY OF CROSS GENDER FRIENDSHIP: The ancient world knew nothing of friendship between the opposite sexes, the medieval world also knew very little. Friendship between the opposite sexes was sanctioned within the context of the new ideal of spiritual friendship in the early Christian communities. The reason for the absence of friendship between the sexes was the subordination of women to men, the separation of male and female spheres, the confinement of women to the roles of daughter, wife and mother. Men and women in traditional society had no opportunity to be friends and no reason to think of one another as potential friends.

EARLY AGE FRIENDSHIP: Boys and girls should be encouraged to mix, of course, with the guidance of an adult. We all know it is often not happening since many cultures simply do not allow it. If it is acceptable, it should be impressed upon the children whether being male or female, they are both humans created differently but uniquely and worthy of respect from each other. Friendship between the sexes will break barriers like the lack of self-esteem and shyness, as they are assured that there is nothing to fear and someone can love them just the way they are, therefore, eventually women will understand men and vice versa. Allow such good principles to be etched on their little hearts, so that when they grow older they will learn to look beyond what they see on the outside and start to look at a woman not as an object of man's pleasure, but as an individual who can make a contribution to the world. In reverse the lady should not to look at a man as a source of life, but more as an individual who also has a mission to accomplish on the planet. At the end of the day, we will have more confident adults living in this world.

THEY SIT, EAT AND LAUGH: While some argue that the mixing of boys and girls is responsible for teenage pregnancy and even higher divorce rates later on in life, I personally think this is not the case. In my humble opinion, if men and women learn to respect each other from an early age, they become better human beings and have stronger relationships. In school you can find that it easier to study with someone of the opposite sex and share ideas and do projects together. Women that have had to work among men in male -dominated environments, also tend to excel so much better as each day is a challenge to prove to their male peers they can also perform better. In such environments, there is neither a male nor female domination as these differences just tend to become invisible. They sit, eat laugh and play together like brothers and sisters and I think this is awesome.

JUST FRIENDS: Can men and women be 'Just Friends,' or is sexual attraction between the genders always inevitable? According to American orthodox Rabbi Shmuley, men and women can be friends with each other as long as they follow certain rules. He talks about platonic friendship between the sexes and shares his ground rules for opposite-sex friendship outside of marriage. If a person isn't married, Rabbi Shmuley says; it's perfectly all right to have friends who are members of the opposite sex. Society has moved away from polarizing the sexes and, today, men and women work together, go to school together and should be able to be friends.

Things are different if you are married, Rabbi Shmuley says. It is possible to have an opposite sex friendship, but you cannot compromise certain borders e.g. You can't have late night dinners together, but you can have lunch together in a public place, but you should not order alcoholic beverages. The embers of attraction really can grow in situations like that, and, suddenly, it's not so innocent, it's not just friendship anymore. You can't take long drives or long flights with the other person, even if it's for work. Even if you have to work with a colleague of the opposite sex, there are still certain human and professional boundaries you need to preserve. You can't place yourself in any situation where romance can grow. Romance grows when people are alone, and romance grows when people share secrets.

MARRIED AS FRIENDS: I know it doesn't sound fair, but married men or women simply cannot be friends with the opposite sex. It is not impossible or impractical. Nothing is wrong with married people wanting opposite - sex friends, but you have to ask yourself if you can you handle the responsibility that comes with the relationship? We always believe we can handle the temptation until we discover that we can't, when it's often too late. Remember what Jesus said about adultery;

"You have heard that it was said, 'Do not commit adultery.'But I tell you that anyone who looks at a woman lustfully has already committed adultery with her in his heart." (Matthew 5: 27-28)

THE DANGER IN HAVING OPPOSITE SEX FRIENDS: Having an opposite-sex friend can put you in danger of both emotional and sexual infidelity. Sometimes spending time with a friend can lead you down the road of relying on them in the way that you should rely on your spouse. Having that emotional closeness to another person could result in you feeling emotionally closer to your friend than your spouse, letting down your guard, and allowing an emotional affair that, even worse, might lead to a physical affair, buying expensive and romantic gifts and in turn changing your attitude towards your partner and expecting them to easily accept that 'we are just friends.' If you are just friends, then it's better to open and just good friends with full transparency.

PROTECT AND VALUE YOUR MARRIAGE: Married people have to take responsibility for protecting their marriage. You have to use every defence mechanism you have to keep your marriage out of harm's way. Infidelity can ruin a marriage, so if avoiding opposite- sex friendship is the cost of staying happily married, it's the best solution. Of course marriage should mean that nothing will happen between two friends, however, so many affairs start innocently with two people who thought they were just going to be friends. They think that all they are doing is having innocent little phone conversations, that as long as they are not having sex, everything is fine. Again, see the words of Jesus quoted above in Matthew 5: 27-28.

Remember there are many changes and sacrifices that you have to make in the interest of keeping a happy home. Managing your friends doesn't mean cutting them off. It just means making sure that you balance the relationship with your marriage and that you don't do anything with that person that you wouldn't want your spouse to do. If you need to deceive your spouse, you have simply overstepped the boundaries of friendship.

There really isn't much that you get from a friend of the opposite sex, that you can't already get from your partner, bearing in mind your partner should be your best and closest friend! So, is what you stand to gain worth more than what you stand to lose? Success in life is about choices, so if you are going to choose marriage, keep your eyes on the prize; 'your spouse.'

PLATONIC FRIENDSHIP:

"As Jesus and His disciples were on their way, he came to a village where a woman named Martha opened her home to him. She had a sister called Mary, who sat at the Lord's feet listening to what he said. But Martha was distracted by the preparations that had to be made. She came to him and asked, 'Lord, don't you care that my sister has **left** *me to do the work by myself? Tell her to help me!' 'Martha, Martha,' the Lord answered. 'You are worried and upset about many things, but only one thing is needed. Mary has chosen what is better and it will not be taken away from her." (Luke 10: 38-41)*

This is the ancient picture of platonic friendship. Martha means 'Lady of the house.' These sisters knew Jesus well. They were close friends with Him, and shared several important episodes in His life. The stories about Martha, Mary and Jesus stake a claim to true platonic friendship.

PLATONIC HISTORY: Platonic friendship is named after a Greek Philosopher, Plato. Plato did not invent the term or the concept that bears his name, but he did see sexual desire as germs for higher loves. Marsilio Ficino, a follower of Plato, used the term amor Socraticus and amor Platonicus interchangeably, for a love between two humans that was preparatory for the love of God. From Ficino's usage, Platonic came to be used for a spiritual love between people of opposite sexes. In our own century, Platonic has been used to describe the relationship which is intimate and affectionate but not sexual, which can apply to members of the same or opposite sex. Though the concept related to same sex is an elevated one, the term has, perhaps, more often been applied in ways that led the 18th century English writer, Samuel Richardson to have one of his characters in his well known book 'Pamela' say, "I am convinced, and always was that Platonic love was chiefly between an older man and a younger; like Socrates and his student Alcibiaden."

PLATONIC AFFECTION: Today, when people refer to platonic love, they refer to an affectionate relationship without sexual intimacy. The type of love Plato seems to have admired most was that in which one man loved another because of his intelligence or virtue, rather than because of his physical attraction. A Platonic friendship refers to a friendship without any sexual implications. Everybody has experienced this type of relations right from the primary school, college, office and even in old age after retiring from active service. This term is generally used to explain the friendship between a man and a woman, without any sexual relationship. Platonic relations can have many forms and types and are hard to realise by others and, sometimes, even by those who are involved in them. The term 'Platonic friend' is, in these days, misunderstood and rarely used in its proper sense, those who are involved can have a lot of feelings for the other person like attachment, affinity, compassion, jealousy or passion. It is very hard to delineate the fine line between them, which is why most of the time; platonic love is confused with some other types of feelings.

PLATONIC CHALLENGES: Just like any other relationship, platonic relationships have got their own challenges. It can be very hard to maintain a platonic relationship without having some feeling for your friend. The more time you spend with the opposite sex the more you grow to love and appreciate them. You might even start seeing them as attractive and start having imaginations of how the two of you would look if you were together. You might even go ahead and ask your platonic friend if you can stop being just friends and start being more involved with each other. Your platonic friends might not take it nicely and you might end up losing a great friendship. If you are married, there is always the danger that your partner might not understand that what you have with your friend is just platonic. They might try to break up your relationship. If you choose not to agree with your spouse, they will constantly fight you. In platonic relationships, you might encounter a problem of drawing a boundary when it comes to sex. This is particularly hard if the two of you are single and your sexual desire is not met. You cannot totally be free to treat a platonic relationship like you would any other friendship. You are left worrying about how your friend will interpret a certain gestures, actions or words. Remember, it takes great vigilance to really keep a platonic relationship innocent.

PLATONIC DEBATE: Many people will tell you that relationship of a non-sexual nature between men and women cannot exist. The argument is based on a number of beliefs that usually focus on one or more persons' sexual attraction to the other. Some say that an attraction, or any thought of a sexual nature, undermines a friendship that a man and woman may think is totally innocent. Here is a heart-searching question: can men and women be just friends? The answer, ultimately, depends on who you ask, and how that person processes their connection with others. Women tend to believe that non-sexual, man-to-woman friendships are possible. The male belief system is often a little less forgiving. To help get a better understanding let's take a look at a few issues and beliefs from both men and women:

HOW MEN SEE IT: Men will openly acknowledge that they lack the self-control to maintain a platonic friendship with a woman, especially an attractive woman. Most men are physically attracted to a female friend who knows how to keep their hands and words to themselves. For a man it can be difficult to maintain a friendship with a woman who is physically appealing. This is when God-fearing, maturity and respect should take precedence. Not surprising, in general, many men seek friendship with women they find sexually attractive. This often results in a stressful situation for men who may find themselves in the company of women they can't have sex with. Of course, the Bible helps fuel this issue. The book of judges shows that male-female friendship usually evolves into romantic flings. It happened between Samson and Delilah. Remember a platonic bond will always be compromised by sexual tension.

HOW WOMEN SEE IT: Women, who designate men into the friend category, don't usually have problems lusting after them, or controlling sexual tension in the relationship. Women tend to develop close friendships with male acquaintances, thereby eliminating the possibility of a romantic encounter. When this happens, women seldom cross the line. Sociologists believe that friendship attraction, devoid of sexual attraction, is a type of bond that men and women can experience. Women believe this, and can separate their physical attraction to a man, if there is one, from their desire to be friends. This is especially true if the man has character flaws or personality differences the woman seeks in an intimate mate.

Since there are predefined feelings or emotions in a male-female friendship, women often choose to be friends with men who make them feel safe. This 'safeness' is defined by women in these situations as:

'This is a male friend with whom I am comfortable because he doesn't view me as a sexual conquest.'

In these instances, a woman may know that she loves her male friend and enjoys his company, but not enough to date or marry him. She usually believes that her male friend thinks the same about her. How wrong she can be!

PLATONIC MAINTENANCE: Is it hard to maintain a platonic friendship? A platonic friendship brings together people of the opposite sex and joins them in the strong bond of friendship. A person does not have to be your boyfriend or girlfriend to be your companion. Opposite sex individuals can share laughs and tears and develop life - long platonic friendships. Here are some simple things to remember:

- ☐ Do not give your friendship any sexual meaning. If you want to be only friends, keep it that way.

- ☐ Do not touch or talk to the person inappropriately.
- ☐ Do not use words with sexual connotations or you risk the friendship delving into 'no go' territories.
- ☐ Keep your feelings in check when people constantly try to imply that the platonic friendship is more that what it seems.
- ☐ Do not let others ruin your relationship with their awkward questions and hidden expectations. Instead, define your own world with your platonic friend.
- ☐ Avoid discussing feminine-masculine-related matters with your male-female platonic friend.
- ☐ Do not treat him or her as your other girlfriends-boyfriends and reserve your judgment until asked.
- ☐ Maintain a high opinion of your platonic friend.
- ☐ Do not undermine his or her intelligence and let them participate in general conversations.
- ☐ Do not mock other men or women in front of them. Be respectful to each other.
- ☐ Avoid being in a situation or position, which can compromise your friendship later on.
- ☐ Do not use unorthodox methods to test your friendship.

- ☐ Appreciate what you have as any false move can push the limits and destroy a beautiful bond.

FRIENDSHIP AND THE BOUNDARIES:

"The western boundary is the coastline of the Great Sea. These are the boundaries around the people of Judah by their clans. In accordance with the Lord's command to him, Joshua gave to Caleb, son of Jephunneh, a portion

in Judah-Kiriath Arba, that is, Hebron." (Joshua 1: 12-13)

You set a boundary they cannot cross; never again will they cover the earth. (Psalm 104: 9)

"Do not move an ancient boundary stone or encroach on the fields of the fatherless, for their defender is strong; He will take up their case against you." (Proverbs 2: 10)

Boundaries are pillars or stones set up to mark the fence of a farm. To remove them, by carrying them to the land of another, was dishonesty and robbery since it was only by that mark that the extent of a man's property could be known. It is forbidden by the Law of Moses for encroaching or intruding upon your neighbor's right or privacy. We are here taught not to invade our friend's right, though we can find ways of doing it ever so secretly and plausibly, clandestinely and by fraud; without any open force. Boundaries are a standing witness to every man's right; let not friendship remove away for then will come wars, and fighting and endless quarreling. The Egyptians said:

'Do not carry off the land mark at the boundaries of arable land, or encroach upon the boundaries of a widow. Removing boundaries meant falsifying the survey and stealing land." "Intruding into your friend's affairs without invitation is removing his boundaries. Respect your friend's right and privacy.'

WHAT ARE BOUNDARIES? A healthy boundary is a space around you that gives a sense of security and safety. Boundaries are very important in all relationships. Social psychologist Jane Adams, PhD, said; "Boundaries regulate distance and closeness, controlling not only how open we are with ourselves from intrusion or encroachment."

You must have some boundaries in order to be respected and valued by your friends as well as yourself. No one respects people that can take advantage of and run over, so to speak. Intimate relationships especially need boundaries to be established. You can only manage your boundaries if you recognize that a boundary issue, either yours or someone else's, exists. What are your boundaries? Have you defined them and clarified them to your friends?

If not, it is time to set some boundaries and then define and explain them to the people and friends that may have an opportunity to cross those boundaries.

WHY BOUNDARIES ARE IMPORTANT: The purpose of having boundaries is to protect and take care of ourselves. We need to be able to tell other people or our friends when they are acting in ways that are not acceptable to us. Healthy boundaries let you choose who you allow into your life, home or family and how they treat you. Healthy boundaries help you figure out who you are, an individual separate from everyone else, and what treatment you will accept. They are also important because they give you a clear sense of who you are. You know which emotions, thoughts, opinions, and feelings are yours when you have boundaries. They help you determine what you will and will not do. The best time to set boundaries is before they are actually needed. It is difficult to know and apply boundaries when someone is insulting or criticizing you. So, do it now and make them clear to avoid misunderstanding and even conflict.

TYPES OF BOUNDARIES: Boundaries are the limit that you set in a relationship to protect yourself from being manipulated by others' needs. They allow you to maintain your individuality, while you share part of your life with another person or your friends. There are five types of boundaries:

1. **Physical boundaries:** You determine who is allowed to touch you and how and when they may touch you. You won't let someone push, kick or hit you, unless you have unhealthy boundaries.

2. **Emotional boundaries:** You determine how many of your feelings you share with others and how many you allow others to share with you in return. Emotional boundaries are important, too. For example, you won't let people insult you, call you names, or tell you where to go if you have healthy boundaries.

3. **Intellectual boundaries:** You determine how you share your ideas and perceptions with others and how you respond to their ideas and their perceptions. It involves knowing that you have a healthy freedom to express your opinion and thoughts without being ridiculed or judged.

4. **Spiritual boundaries:** You determine whom you share your spiritual beliefs with.

5. **Sexual boundaries:** You determine who you share your sexuality with, how and when, including physical activity, jokes and comments etc.

HOW TO SET YOUR BOUNDARIES: The first step to building boundaries around you is to know that you have the right to protect and defend yourself, also it's your duty to take responsibility for how you allow others to Interact with you. Be honest with yourself, figure out what you really, truly think and feel, before you express your true thoughts to others; you need to admit them to yourself. Set boundaries with your loved ones, family members, friends and co-workers. The more clearly defined your boundaries are the better, as they will be received and respected. Say what you mean and mean what you say. Once a boundary is set, and someone crosses it, then there should be consequences of some nature. Let the consequence fit the intrusion.

WHAT ARE THE CONSEQUENCES? It is very important to set consequences that you are willing and able to enforce. If you are setting boundaries in a relationship, and you are not yet at a point where you are ready to leave the relationship. Don't say you will leave, but you should say that you will start considering all of your options, which may include leaving. Don't say you will do something that you are not yet ready or willing to do. To set boundaries and not enforce them just gives the other person an excuse to continue in the same old behavior. Since behavior patterns are quite ingrained in all of us, it is important to allow the other person some room to make a change in behavior, unless the behavior is really intolerable and totally unacceptable. Healthy relationship boundaries are like flexible gates. They allow you to either get close to someone or keep your distance, depending on the appropriateness of the situation. Boundaries become unhealthy when they swing too easily, letting everyone in, or staying rigid, therefore keeping every one out. If you don't establish enough boundaries, you run the risk of letting someone manipulate, abuse or stick to you. By establishing too many boundaries, however, you deny yourself the chance to achieve true intimacy.

CHAPTER 7

WHEN FRIENDSHIP HURTS

"If an enemy were insulting me, I could endure it; if a foe were raising himself against me, I could hide from him. But it is you, a man like myself, my companion, my close friend, with whom I once enjoyed sweet fellowship as we walked with the throng at the house of God." (Psalm 55: 12-14)

In the city, all kinds of passion had broken loose, King David's friend had taken part in this hostile rising. It was not an open enemy, who might have had cause that opposed to him, but faithless friends and, among them was 'Ahithophel,' his counselor and best friend. Ahithophel, the friend of David was the ringleader of the conspirators that misrepresented him and his government. *(See 2 Samuel 15: 31 & 1 Chronicles 27: 33).*

There always has been, and always will be, a mixture of good and bad, sound and unsound friends. We must not be surprised if we are sadly deceived by some that have made great pretension to friendship. Unfaithfulness puts friendship out of joint. Selfishness rends each from the other, and disjoints the whole frame of society and friendship. Passion and ill will breaks every band of friendship and gratitude. There is no real trust in any, all are corrupt. It is better to trust in the Lord than to put your confidence in man.

FRIENDSHIP IS DYING: There is no faith in man; people have grown so treacherous that one does not know whom to have confidence in. You will not meet a friend that you dare trust, whose word you dare take, or who will show any tenderness or concern for you, so that wise men shall take it for a rule. Society, and friendship, is dying gradually at its roots and the enemies of man are those of his own surroundings. Suspicion, distrust and enmity are prevailing among good friends. Considering the modern world, human nature has changed. The law of friendship is also changing, where are the good friends? What type of friend are you? Who is your friend? Who can you really depend on?

There is no prediction that friendship will turn out to be a reliable, positive relationship in your life or, by contrast, that a negative association will cause you emotional distress, or worse. Since destructive or negative friends are not always that easy to spot, being forewarned is being forearmed, as the saying goes. Some friends may be betrayers from the start; others may turn into betrayers because of what is going on in their lives, or because of changes in their personality. Sometimes you need to consider what your friend is really like within the context of all the behaviors. Here are six traits to consider, that could pose problems in friendship:

1. THE PROMISE BREAKER: This type of friend constantly disappoints you or breaks promises, most likely because he was constantly disappointed during his formative years. Your friend is unable to stop himself from repeating that behavior. It is an annoying but comfortable behavior for your friend and, without psychological help, it may be hard for them to stop this behavior. You could stay away from the friend and the friendship, or you could find a way to detach yourself by lowering your expectation from this friendship. If they promise to do something for you, even to meet you for lunch, you can say "Sure," but protect yourself by knowing, at the back of your mind, that this person will disappoint you more often than not.

Although your friend may always have been this way, they may also have recently acquired this unreliability because of something they are going through. If a friend who has always been there for you, through thick and thin, has only recently become less reliable, you might want to cut them some slack. You have to decide if this is a life-long trait that will be hard or impossible to change, a temporary condition that will be short-lived, or something, if it does continue indefinitely, that you are willing to accept and handle.

One way to try to help or change the Promise Breaker is to help them to understand the consequence of their ignored pledges. Perhaps you have been keeping your disappointment about this to yourself. Try telling them how it makes you feel. If you want to continue your friendship with them, make sure you reconfirm any plans, at least once or even right before you are supposed to meet. If you have a mobile phone or pager, make sure your friend is able to contact you so won't, at least, be left waiting if, they cancel a meeting once more. If their unreliability is out of character, then maybe it's a time for you to be a real friend and explore the reason(s) by offering an ear to listen.

2. THE DOUBLE CROSSER:

"After He had said this, Jesus was troubled in spirit and testified, 'I tell you the truth, one of you is going to betray me." (John 13: 21)

Judas, a professed friend, betrayed the blessed Lord. It is a sign of ingratitude to betray a friend. Those in whom you repose confidence may turn to betray you. Friends who have received from you great favors or those you have helped, protected and nourished may turn against you, expose and deliver you up into the hands of your enemies. Double-crossing is betraying or cheating an associate. This negative friend betrays you big-time. It could happen when someone does something to hurt you, such as spreading a malicious rumor about you. Or, it could be an emotional double-crossing, for example, when a close or best friend stops speaking to you and you never find out why. The double-crosser may have some real emotional issues that need to be addressed if you are to continue the friendship. If your friend was betrayed by a parent or sibling during their formative years, they may have a habit to repeat that behavior with friends. The betrayal could have been as subtle as being disappointed by a parent or as blatant as being the victim of emotional, physical or sexual abuse. Your friend may need an outsider i.e. counselor or pastor, to help reverse the cycle of doing to others what has been done to them. If you have been double-crossed by a particular friend, you may want to consider ending the friendship. If you have not been directly harmed by this friend but have evidence that they have hurt others, you have to decide if you are risking too much by maintaining the friendship. If you do decide to walk away from this friendship, do it in a low-key or wise way that avoids incurring the anger of the double-crosser, so you do not become the next victim. The Lord Jesus Christ dealt wisely with Judas, though he was a double-crosser, i.e. betrayer.

3. THE SELF ABSORBED: Self-absorbed is also called self-centered. So self absorbed friends focus more on themselves than on others. They can be charming and at first their stories may be interesting and even entertaining, but listening to them talk on and on about themselves can be draining. If his friend does not put his needs out, they are in big trouble as the self-centered friend has unrealistic expectations of others and will manipulate to cater for their every need, they are also easily offended. When things don't go their way they can be verbally and physically abusive and make makes others responsible for their feelings having a total lack of empathy for others, while constantly shifting blame to others for their problems and mistakes. Their personality is often different in the public from the one in private. Simply, their opinion counts for everything as the feel they have the final authority and are entitled to be treated differently from others. Furthermore, they are generally uncooperative and act acts superior while craving for adoration. Many people have self-centered people as friends which they cannot avoid. Try the following ideas for dealing with them so your energy does not get drained.

***Stay focused internally*:** Self-absorbed friends suck the energy out of others by being the center of attention. They want others' ears and eyes on them, so keep part of your focus on your breathing, and emotions and don't surrender to it and you will feel less drained.

Stay in a group: Within a group of people there is bound to be general interaction, which can prevent the self-centered friend from engaging everyone's attention. So, make sure there is at least one other person around when you interact with your self-centered friend.

Discover their underlining needs: Underneath self-absorption is the need for attention and approval. What message might help fill this person's need so they can relax in the conversation, perhaps some time or acknowledgement?

Be careful what you promise: Some self-centered friends have a tendency to ask for favours and expect others to bend over backwards for them. Promise only what you can and are willing to deliver and don't take responsibility for their neediness.

Set clear boundaries: Define your boundaries by deciding when, where and how much time to spend together. Choose the time to get together when you feel strong and energized. Have a back-up plan for when it's time to leave. Learn how to say 'no' without feeling guilty.

4. THE COMPETITOR:

"We do not dare to classify or compare ourselves with some who commend themselves. When they measure themselves by themselves and compare themselves with themselves, they are not wise.
We, however, will not boast beyond proper limits, but will confine our boasting, as even to you."
(2 Corinthians 10: 12-13)

A little bit of competition is healthy and to be expected. An appropriate amount of competition will motivate and stimulate, but too much competition between friends can destroy the friendship. One of the primary ingredients in a positive friendship is that one or both friends feel they can be themselves and they don't have to put on 'airs and graces' or need to impress one another. Competition implies a race in which one wins and the other loses, those conditions are quite the opposite of what someone typically expects in a positive friendship, especially a close one. Friends who are competitors probably compete in every area of their lives and find it difficult or impossible to ease up, even when they are with close friends. They may compete at work, school, church, sport and in the community affairs, as these competitors put themselves forward, and boast of their achievements and attainments. They look at their own accomplishments, but do not look at the excellence of others. They form a great opinion of themselves, and undervalue all others. This is a description of pride and self-complacency. How many there are, and it is feared, even among professing true friends, who secretly, in their hearts and actions, compete with their friends. They look on themselves as the true measure of greatness and condemn all others, however excellent these may be, who differ from them. They see their character, habits, achievements, family, house, car, job, etc, through their own eyes as being perfect, and see little or no greatness in others. True friends should not act like such this; they should stay away from the society of unwise self - approved competitors who are, really, neither wise nor true friends.

5. THE FAULT FINDER:

"And when they saw some of His disciples eat bread with unwashed hands, they found fault." (Mark 7: 2)

To find fault means to censure or blame. A fault finder is a person who complains about or criticizes everything another does. Nothing you do, say, or wear is good enough for this critical friend. They would probably have been raised by extremely judgmental parents, who were also equally hypercritical siblings. Faultfinding is a character trait difficult to accept and your friend may even be unaware that they are critical of others and they annoy or upsets them. Before labeling this type of friendship as hopelessly destructive, you might want to find out if your friend could recognize this behavior in you or you in them, and with time, help you and/or them to drop it. Otherwise, you may just have to accept this trait in yourself or your friend, knowing that it reflects on character and not necessarily on friendship.

If you value your relationship with a fault finding friend and want to maintain the friendship, in spite of their criticisms, try sharing with them how their behavior affects you. Discuss how they affect you and try to help them. This will help you to be less resentful and more accommodating to your friend. However, if you are at your wit's end and willing to try one more thing before calling it quits, try finding faults with them. Those who criticize and find faults are often unable to hear this about them from others. Criticizing them may break their spell of negativity; however, they might cut off your friendship forever rather than face up to your criticisms, or try to come to terms with your assessment of their character. So, be aware of the risks.

6. TYPES OF 'TOXIC' FRIENDS - LISTED:

The Phoney: This is a friend who pretends to be something they are not.
The User: A friend who uses you for their own purposes and goals.
The Thief: A friend who constantly borrows or takes your things and never returns them.
The Betrayer: A friend who double-crosses you in very step you take.
The Promise Breaker: A friend who always breaks their promises. This friend is unreliable.
The Dare-devil: A friend who takes unnecessary risks that can endanger your circumstances.
The Cheat: A friend who steals or messes around with your romantic partner.
The Gossip: A friend who discloses your secrets or private affairs.
The Abuser: A friend who abuses you verbally, physically, sexually and emotionally.
The Self-centered: A friend who is only concerned with their own wants and needs.
The Competitor: A friend who wants everything you have and will try and take it from you.
The Fault-finder: A friend who is extremely critical and finds faults with everything you do.
The Copy Cat: A friend, who imitates everything you do and wants to be like you.
The Regulator: A friend wants to control everything about your friendship.
The Snob: A friend who disrespects you and lets you knows it.

The Reliant: A friend who overly depends on you and is extremely needy.
The Shrink: A friend who analyses everything you do and constantly offers pieces of advice.
The Con-artist: A friend who steals from you by subtle deception or 'friendly fraud.'
The Care-taker: A friend, who acts like your parent and assumes to be your babysitter or keeper.
The Interposer: A friend who selfishly interferes with every aspect of your life.
The Miserable: A friend who is always sad and unhappy and tries to make you feel the same.
The One-upper: A friend who is always trying to be one up on you.
The Loner: A friend who prefers to be alone than with you or other friends.
The Accuser: A friend who blames you for all the problems in their life.
The Lazy Bone: A friend, who is extremely lazy, constantly wanting you to do things for them.
The Stalker: A friend who invades your personal space without your permission.
The Liar: A friend who constantly lies to you and tries to justify each lie.
The Envious: A friend who is extremely jealous of you and what you have and do.
The Arrogant: A friend who thinks they are better than you and is extremely proud.
The Know-It-All: A friend who thinks they are an expert in everything and tries to undermine you.
The Drama King or Queen: A friend who is full of drama, and tries to make you part of it.

The Passive/Aggressive: A friend who uses non-verbal actions to let you know they are upset.
The Jekyll and Hyde: A friend who is moody and nasty one day and nice and exuberant the next.
The Houdini: A friend who always finds a clever way to get out of something.
The Bully: A friend who intimidates you with devious actions, manipulations and verbal insults.
The Runner: A friend who runs from the truth, responsibilities, confrontations and commitments.
The Doctor: A friend who diagnosis your ailments and suggests a treatment.
The defender: A friend who won't let you fight your own battle.
The doomed: A pessimistic friend who is always negative about everything.
The Whiner: A friend who acts like a child in an adult's body and is always complaining.
The Gas Lighter: A friend who tries to confuse your perceptions, making you think you are crazy.
The Guilt-Monger: A friend who tries to make you feel guilty about everything you do or say.
The Procrastinator: A friend who puts off until tomorrow what they could do today.
The Religious Hypocrite: A friend who thinks they are holier and more faithful than you.
The Piney Pincher: A friend who is cheap and thrifty not wanting to spend their own money.
The Attention Seeker: A friend who wants to be the center of attraction all the time.
The Perfectionist: A friend who is very rigid, inflexible and demands a lot from you.

The Chamber: A friend who pretends to be the nicest person you've ever met, until they show you their true colour.

Quite a long list! Do you indentify with any of these traits in yourself or others?

PEOPLE DON'T REALLY SEE TOXIC FRIENDS: I suspect that toxic friendship can drain a person more than anything else, because other sources of stress are easier to identify, while most of the time people don't really see when a friend is draining the life, soul and happiness out of them. These signs can apply to both men and women. A toxic friend talks about everybody, their neighbor is stupid, their cousins are fat, his or her co- workers are nosey; did you hear that (our friend) is getting a divorce? Here is a clue, if your friend gossips about everyone else don't think they are not gossiping about you. Their world is always worse than yours. You mention how you were late to an important meeting because you forgot to fill up the tank, then you had to stop and get gas, a toxic friend tells you that's nothing. Your positives are his negatives. You just got a promotion and your toxic friend doesn't congratulate you, instead they points out how you'll have to work more and you probably didn't get that much of a raise. They mention how others at work will probably hate you because you are now their boss. Toxic friends are friends who make a joke of insults. However, they will tell you not to worry as they were just joking with you because they love you. Your other friends refuse their company and question why you are their friend. It is true that sometimes our best friends can pre-judge people; the fact still remains that those outside of the situation can see it more clearly than those standing right in the middle of it.

LOVE YOUR ENEMY:

"It is easy enough to be friendly to one's friends. But to befriend the one who regards him or herself as your enemy is the evidence of true religion. The other is mere business."
(Mahatma Gandhi 1869-1948 - prominent leader of Indian Nationalism)

Whether or not, you are a Christian, there's something in the teachings of the Lord Jesus Christ that is worth contemplating. For anyone who seeks to be a better person, just heed his urging that we love our enemies.

"But I tell you who hear me; love your enemies, do good to those who hate you. Bless those who curse you, and pray for those who mistreat you" (Luke 6: 27-28)

All obedience begins with affection, as nothing is done right unless love is the motivation. Man is a creature created out of love; therefore is love not the way?

"We love because he first loved us." (1 John 4: 19-21)

Jesus' only commandment was to love others as He loves us.

"And this is his command: to believe In the name of his son, Jesus Christ, and to love one another as he commanded us. Those who obey his commands live in him and he in them. And this is how we know that he lives in us: We know it by the Spirit he gave us." (1 John 3: 23-24)

Who's Your Friend?

Love is a short and sweet word, yet it is the rest and satisfaction of the soul. Love was the heart of the Savior's teachings, because it is the essence of the character of God. There are two kinds of love, involving the same general feeling or springing from the same fountain of goodwill. One is that feeling by which we approve of the conduct of another, commonly called the love of complacency; the other, is that we wish well to the person or another, though we cannot approve of their lifestyle. This is the love of benevolence, and this love we are to bear towards our enemies. It is impossible to love the conduct of a person who curses and reviles us, who injures our person or property, or who violates all the laws of God; but, though we may hate their conduct, and suffer keenly when we are affected by it, yet we may still wish them well and pity their madness and folly. Furthermore, we may speak kindly of and to them and return good for evil, offering them aid in times of trial, seeking to do good and to promote their eternal welfare.

Do not repay anyone evil for evil. Be careful to what is right in the eyes of everybody. If it is possible, as far as it depends on you, live at peace with everyone. Do not take revenge, my friends, but leave room for God's wrath, for it is written: "It is mine to avenge; I will repay," says the Lord.
On the contrary: "If your enemy is hungry, feed him; if he is thirsty, give him something to drink. In doing this, you will heap burning coals on his head." Do not be overcome by evil, but overcome evil with good. (Romans 12: 17-21)

This seems to be what is meant by loving our enemies; and this is a special law of Christianity, and is the highest possible test of piety, and probably the most difficult of all duties to be performed.

THE GREATEST CHALLENGE: Not just "Love your neighbor," which, in itself can be a difficult thing, but "love your enemies." That is a powerful message and it turns out to be one of the greatest challenges in life. Why is this message so important, even if you're not a Christian? I am not here to discuss Christian teachings, but to address universal problems found in every human being, no matter what your religion or those without any faith. This is a universal problem! The hatred we feel for other people, the hatred that wells up inside of us causing destructive actions, for people who might have harmed us in some way but in the end are fellow human beings, who we must live with in a common society.

This still might sound a bit grand or preachy, so let me bring this down to an everyday level. Is there anyone in your life who you detest, hate or just can't abide? Maybe someone who just irritates you, or a person who you resent and feel bitterness towards, if so, are you proud of those feelings? Do they make you happy? I believe that most of us have someone like that, and in many cases multiple people in our lives that cause us anger or hatred or at least resentment, maybe for something they have done in the past. I also believe this anger, hatred and resentment we harbor within us are destructive and counterproductive.

WHAT DOES TO LOVE YOUR ENEMY REALLY MEAN? Well, it is probably pretty self-explanatory, but I think it is necessary to clarify. Your enemy does not just mean the enemy of your nation, community or neighbor. I am not talking necessarily about terrorists, criminals or bullies. I am talking about people you generally dislike, in any way. Who are these people? Maybe, someone who has picked on you or called you names or disrespected you in some way causing you anger? Maybe, you just hold a grudge against someone? Maybe a family member you have had a big fight with? It could be someone you have been angry at for some time, or a person who did something horrible to a loved one, even a co-worker, boss or friend who is mean to you. There are a whole range of emotions and reasons.

What does it mean to love these people? Obviously it is non-romantic love, but there are different kinds of non-romantic love. There is the love you have for your parents, your children, your siblings, your best friend; all of these are different in some way. Then there's the love you have for someone who just did something wonderful for you, whether that's someone you know or a complete stranger. There is the love for your fellow human being; this is the love I mean. Have you felt non-sexual, non-romantic love for another who is not even a family member or a very close friend? Maybe, they did something really nice for you or another person. Maybe you are just feeling really good about humanity right now, for whatever reason, this is an incredible person who inspires you or changes lives by volunteering to help the powerless.

PUT ASIDE THE WRONG AND TURN THE OTHER CHEEK: To 'love your enemy,' is to find it in your heart to put aside any wrongs, and to love them as a fellow human being. You don't have to love them like you love parents, siblings, children or your best friend. Just have loving feelings towards them, and if possible, express it through words, or by doing something nice, or simply with a smile. It is not easy, I know. Think about this as a challenge and picture the person you dislike most, and see if it is easy to find that love for them. Imagine someone who murdered someone you love. That would certainly be an 'enemy.' Could you find it in your heart to forgive and love that person? I know that would be the most difficult thing in my entire life, which brings up the question: 'Why should I?'

"The hunger for love is much more difficult to remove than the hunger for bread." (Agnes Gonxha Bojaxhiu 1910-1997 'Mother Teresa')

WHY SHOULD I LOVE MY ENEMY?

"Love is the only force capable of transforming an enemy into a friend." (Dr Martin Luther King Jnr)

It might sound too corny for many of you, and, if so, you might not even be reading this by now. That is ok. This idea might not be for everyone. After all, this person, my 'enemy,' has done something horribly wrong to me, why on earth would I want to love them? What do I get out of it? This isn't an easy question to answer, and I won't be able to explore all the possible answers, that would require a book. But let's look briefly at a few reasons:

YOU WILL BE HAPPIER: If you have anger or resentment inside of you, even if you don't think about it all the time, there will be times when it will surface. When it does it makes you unhappy. It is destructive, inwardly and consumes you both inwardly and outwards. You might be tempted to do destructive things to others. That anger also affects others around you, such as your loved ones, who are most likely affected in some way when you are angry, even if the anger is not directed at them. Removing this anger from yourself is a positive thing, and it will make you happier overall.

YOU COULD CHANGE THAT PERSON'S LIFE: Your enemy is a human being, and it is very possible that your hatred of that person is a source of grief, tension, or hatred in them. Now, that might feel good to you in a vindictive way, but if you look at it objectively, removing your feelings from the situation, hurting another person is always a bad thing. Making them happier is a good thing. Interestingly, making someone happy can make us happier, no matter, who that person is.

YOU COULD MAKE A NEW FRIEND: One of the most powerful effects of learning to love your enemy is that your enemy can become your friend. While it is counterproductive to be fighting with an enemy, as it hinders your progress, it is also very productive to add new friends to your life, and they can help you accomplish things. A new friend, instead of an enemy, makes an incredible difference, also, if that enemy happens to be a family member or former friend, reuniting can be extremely powerful, important and positive experience.

YOU CAN SET A BETTER EXAMPLE TO OTHERS: Our actions set an example for other people in our lives. If you have children, for example, they learn from much from what you do and how you achieve it. Teaching them to hate and be angry is not a positive example, but teaching them to overcome that anger and hate, and to forgive and make up with an enemy, while showing love, there is no better example in life.

IT IS BETTER FOR THE SOCIETY: This is obvious to me, but it is important to say. One relationship might not seem to make a difference to society as a whole. I mean, who really cares if I dislike or even hate another person? But, if you think of it this way, what if we all carry hate for another person? It means everyone is either hating or being hated, so by definition creates a divisive, fractured and angry society. I see the effects of this everywhere, from media, culture, politics, through business and families; all being disrupted. Therefore, this idea brings an opportunity because the opposite must be true, so, if we can overcome that hatred, and learn to love our neighbor and our enemy, society is better off in so many ways.

IT TESTS YOUR CHARACTER AS A PERSON: This might not be important, but for me it is. I like to think of myself as a good person, but how good am I if I just love my family and friends? That is usually extremely easy to do, but a better test of your goodness is if you can overcome feelings of resentment and hate and turn them into feelings of respect and love. That is a true challenge, but as stated earlier it was a command from Jesus, in fact the only real command he gave, so It's plain to see the importance.

MAKING AN ENEMY TO BECOME A FRIEND:

"You have heard that it was said, 'Love your neighbor and hate your enemies,' but I tell you: love your enemies and pray for those who persecute you, that you may be sons of your Father in heaven." (Matthew 5: 44)

Who's Your Friend?

"Bless those who persecute you; bless and do not curse." (Romans 12: 14)
Do not repay anyone evil for evil. Be careful to what is right in the eyes of everybody. If it is possible, as far as it depends on you, live at peace with everyone. Do not take revenge, my friends, but leave room for God's wrath, for it is written: "It is mine to avenge; I will repay," says the Lord. On the contrary: "If your enemy is hungry, feed him; if he is thirsty, give him something to drink. In doing this, you will heap burning coals on his head." Do not be overcome by evil, but overcome evil with good. (Romans 12: 17-21)

Since men became enemies to God, they have been found to be enemies of one another. There Is an old saying ' divide and rule,' which is what started with the fall of man, which is why Jesus Christ came and commanded us to love others, even those who do us harm, and to do good to them that hate us; So, if your enemy is needy in any way, do good to them, and supply their need. The way to bring your enemy to repentance and make them a friend is to show the person love. On this principle God is acting continually. He does well to all, even to the rebellious, and He designs that His goodness should lead people to repentance. People will resist anger and power; but cannot resist 'goodness,' it finds its way to their heart; and works on the conscience. If people will act on this principle, the world would be at peace and a far safer and happier experience. Whoever are your enemies that wish you ill and seek to do you ill, your rule is to do them no hurt, but all the good you can.

A BAD RETURN FOR YOUR ACTIONS:

"Do not repay anyone evil for evil." *(Romans 12: 17).*

To retaliate is a bad return for your actions. God does so much for His enemies, much more than we know. Christ died for us when we were sinners 'Enemies of God.' *(See: Romans 5: 8-10)* So do not let the evil provocation from your enemy have power over you or make such an impression upon you, as to dispossess you of yourself. An 'eye for an eye' will disturb your peace, destroy your love, discompose your spirits, transport you into any indecencies, and bring you to consider or attempt revenge.
"He that cannot quietly bear the injury of his or her enemy is perfectly conquered by it." (Exposition from Romans 12 by Matthew Henry, J.B Williams, Joseph Hughes)

"An eye for an eye will make the whole world blind."
(Mahatma Gandhi 1869-1948 - prominent leader of Indian Nationalism)

Therefore, learn to defeat your enemy's ill plan against you, and to seek to change them by doing them good from the bottom of your heart.

"He that has this rule over his or her spirit is better than the mighty." (Proverbs 16: 32)

We cannot deal with a man as an adversary over whom we are to seek to gain a victory, but as an erring human being. There is the great danger that when you undertake the work of punishment, you would forget the so-called 'enemy' is a fellow human being. Why, therefore, treat and regard them as an enemy? We set ourselves in array against them, and consider them at once as enemies of our lives, and as having lost all claims to sympathy. The Lord Jesus said; "the enemy is your fellow human being, he or she is to be followed with tender sympathy and prayer, and the heart and arm of brotherhood." How can this be done? How can you make your enemy your friend?

DETACH YOURSELF: When you think about your 'enemy,' you most likely have feelings of anger or something along those lines. Instead of letting those feelings overcome you and determine your actions, stop yourself. Be aware of your feelings. See if you can detach yourself from them and see your 'enemy' more as a victim of evil powers or influences and fellow human being. Think about forgiveness and gently remove yourself from the situation.

"You are wise if few things annoy you." Arnold Bennett - English writer (1867-1931)

PUT YOURSELF IN THEIR SHOES: Now that you have removed yourself from the situation, try being in the other person's head and body. Imagine yourself becoming that person, what are they like from the inside? How did they get to be that person they are? What have they been through?
Why would they have done what they did? How do they feel about it? Imagine them as a real human being, not just someone who is evil and done wrong. All people try to do good things, but they make often make mistakes, or have a different perspective. Seeing the situation from the other person's perspective is very difficult, but very important.

'Don't express pity, take action.' 'Don't give advice, set an example.'

The colour of the sink is not the mark of the man. We have nothing to do with, nor can we blame the creator of mankind for it. Go beyond that and see a fellow human being. Thousands of people have committed suicide because of mental depression caused by rejection.
Try putting yourself in their shoes.

SEEK TO UNDERSTAND: Understanding forms the basis of all things we do in relation to other people. Without it, we cannot hope to really practice the golden rule towards others, and our relationships cannot really attain the riches and beauty that we are capable of. Understanding others is the objective of putting yourself in their shoes. "Seek and ye shall find," Jesus said. When seeking to understand another person, what are you really doing? You are seeking to comprehend what's important to them. 'Fundamentally, you can understand others by seeking to understand them, so we love others by seeking to love them.' It is important to stress this here, because if you can understand what your enemy, did and why they did it, you can start from the next steps explained below. Really try to understand, even if you don't want to. ***"Understanding is the beginning of acceptance." (Napoleon***
Bonaparte, military leader 1769-1821)

SEEK TO ACCEPT: Instead of fighting the culprit who has hurt you, and wanting them to be different or to do things differently, accept them for who they are. Accept what has happened as a part of life and that things can be different, because it has already happened and you can't change the past, but only the future. Accept that this person can't be different, because that is who they are. This, too, is a very difficult step, but if you cannot accept, you cannot love.

"One road to happiness is acceptance." (Napoleon Bonaparte, military leader 1769-1821)

FORGIVE AND LET THE PAST STAY IN THE PAST: This may be the most difficult step of all. Can you truly forgive this person for what they have done, in your heart? If you have detached yourself and have tried to understand and accepted them for what has happened it should be easier. Try to think this way; what happened is in the past, it cannot be changed. You can either hate what has happened in the past, change nothing and be angry, or accept it and move on. It will do nothing but eat you up or destroy your peace and tranquility. Once you have let go of the past, let go of your feelings about what this person or people have done. Those feelings will do you no good. 'To forgive is the proof of a true hero.' Let it go and move on.

"A wise man will make haste to forgive, because he knows the true value of time." (Dr Samuel Johnson, Author 1709-1784)

"To err is human, to forgive is divine." (Alexander Pope, English poet 1688-1744)

FIND SOMETHING TO LOVE: If you can forgive, and release those bad feelings, you are left with neutrality and you want to replace this with love, but how do you do this? Find something in that person to love Is the answer. It could be anything, their smile, willingness to help someone, generosity, even their stubbornness. Find something admirable, loveable or simply something that is positive. There is something like that in every person; you may need to get to know that person better, which in itself can be difficult. 'Amor vincit omnia,' ('Love conquers all.') There is nothing holier in this life than the first consciousness of love. Love is a power with the potential for goodness. How many injuries will it forgive, what obstacles will it overcome and what sacrifice will it make rather than give up on a fellow human being?

TRY TO SEE THEM AS YOURSELF AND DISCOVER SOME LOVE FOR THEM: If the above steps prove too difficult, it is probably because you don't know that person well enough. Instead, project yourself into them. See them as similar to yourself in some ways, or try to think of them as similar in some way to a loved one and use those similarities to find something to love.

FIND SOME COMMON GROUND: You have things in common with just about everyone, if you look hard enough. That might be a common interest, shared or common experience while growing up or working, people you know or love in common, or with whom you share personality traits. This common ground will help you relate to that person better.

OPEN YOUR HEART: This is another very difficult step, as your heart tends to remain closed to people who have hurt you as a defensive mechanism. You are afraid of being vulnerable, being rejected or hurt. Yet this closing of your heart is what prevents you from loving and receiving love. Even if you are able to open your heart to your loved ones, but no one else, that is limiting yourself. This is a great challenge, and something that really can only happen with practice. Above all, if you want to have a magnetic, attractive personality, cultivate the heart qualities. It is the lovable, not the intellectual qualities, that draw and hold people. You must make people feel your sympathy, feel that they have met or encountered a real man or woman. Do not be afraid to open your heart, fling its door wide open. Meet people, including your enemy with a warm, sincere greeting and an open heart, it will do wonders for you. You will find the stiffness, difference and indifference, the cold lack of interest in everybody, which now so troubles you disappear. The practice of open-heartedness will revolutionise your social power. You will develop attractive and loving qualities, which you never dreamed you would ever possess.

REACH OUT TO THEM: It is one thing to feel love for the person that hurt you, but quite another to express it practically. There are many ways to express love. Of course, some ways you might consider are saying nice things to them, having an open discussion about what has happened and express your feelings, giving them a symbolic hug, doing something nice for them, smiling, cracking a joke, and so on. Life is all about challenges. Have you overcome these challenges?

"Am I not destroying my enemies when I make friends of them?" (Abraham Lincoln, 16th President of USA)

FRIENDSHIP AND BETRAYAL:

"While he was still speaking, Judas, one of the Twelve, arrived. With him was a large crowd armed with swords

and clubs, sent from the chief priest and the elders of the people. Now the betrayer had arranged a signal with them: 'The one I kiss is the man; arrest him.' Jesus replied. Friend, do what you came for." (Matthew 26: 47-50)

To betray is to deliver up to an enemy, to prove faithless to or to disclose secret information. A kiss is a token of all allegiance and friendship. But Judas, when he broke all the laws of love, profaned the lovely sign to serve his purpose. There are many that betray their friends with a kiss, with the pretence of doing themselves honour. 'To embrace is one thing, to love is another?' The Lord Jesus called Judas 'friend,' meaning companion. How this word would have cut into his soul, if he had any sensibility left! What is the human heart not capable of, when it rejects God, and yields to the influence of Satan and the love of money? The Lord Jesus called the betrayer 'friend' to demonstrate and teach us how to show meekness under the greatest betrayal, bitterness and treachery.

PERSONAL CONFIDANTE: True friends are hard to find. Most of the time, people end up with the wrong people and find it difficult to adjust to them. With the increasing selfishness and strenuous competition between peers, arises the difficulty in finding a friend one could blindly trust and look up to in times of need. Also, with the increasing interest of people in gossip and cheap plots, betrayal of friendship has become very common.

"If an enemy were insulting me, I could hide from him. But it is you, a man like myself, my companion, my close friend, with whom I once enjoyed sweet fellowship as we walked with the throng at the house of God." (Psalm 55: 12-13)

That which overwhelmed the Psalmist, was the fact that the series of betrayal he faced came from one who had been his friend. The reproach which he felt most keenly came from one whom he regarded as a personal confidante; a friend who he showed love and kindness, and to whom he revealed all his secret feelings. Of all experiences in life, betrayal by a trusted friend is the most difficult to bear. The Psalmist and his friend had worshipped together in the house of God, but now he has joined the enemies. Betrayal by a close friend is devastating. It produces a feeling of worthlessness for having trusted an untrustworthy person. It raises questions about our judgment. Because of the intimate friend's knowledge of our situation, such betrayal has a great potential for further damage.

LET IT GO: The betrayed Psalmist turned to God for intervention, but with what language. He cursed them to go down alive to Sheol. Jeremiah also prayed that his enemy would not succeed and that his eternal dishonor would never be forgotten. *(See: Jeremiah 20: 11)* Can we do better, even in the extremity of betrayal by a friend? We can perhaps not rid ourselves of our negative emotions, but we can remember that revenge is always counterproductive. Betrayal is part of life and few of us are fortunate enough to make it through life unaffected by it. Betrayal by a trusted friend is a deeply painful experience. It is hard to imagine what a friend might possibly gain by stabbing you in the back. Some friends might make things up in an attempt to ruin your reputation. These are those who betray a confidence and reveal secrets to set off rumors and gossip. The pain of such an experience can be overwhelming. Learning how to deal with the experience is an important prerequisite for moving on. And how you choose to deal with it will determines the relationship between you and the friend who wronged you. The word 'forgiveness' means 'to let go.' If you can let go of such experiences, you can move beyond your betrayal. Coping with a broken friendship is quite hard, more so, if you are innocent. But, life goes on and you make new friends. You push away your hurtful past and learn a valuable lesson from it.

'Betrayal is the willful slaughter of hope.'

HANDLING A JEALOUS FRIEND:

"Then he dreamed still another dream and told it to his brothers, and said I have dreamed another dream…so he told it to his father and his brothers; and his father rebuked him and said to him, 'What is this dream that you have dreamed? And his brothers envied him, but his father kept the matter in mind." (Genesis 37: 9–11)

Jacob's sons were inflamed with jealousy to hear from Joseph's lips, the suggestion that he would rule over them. He, the young favoured prince, evidently believed that he would have pre-eminence over the entire family. In his guileless talk, he stirred up all the fires of jealousy and murderous hatred. Yet God did have in mind some wondrous blessings for the young Joseph.

WHAT IS JEALOUSY? Jealousy is a resentful envy of someone's success, achievement, advantages or possessions etc. Envy and jealousy are closely related, however, with slight difference in connotation. Envy connotes a longing to possess something awarded to or achieved by another. Jealousy, on the other hand, connotes a feeling of resentment towards another that has gained something that they believe they more rightfully deserve. Jealousy also refers to pain caused by fear of losing someone or something to a rival. Jealousy kills love, as ashes smothers the flame. Jealousy can feed on bitterness, no less than that which is sweet, and is sustained by pride as often as by affection. Jealousy can be healthy or unhealthy, depending on your motivation. Unhealthy jealousy stems from fear, insecurity, deception, or covetousness. A jealous disposition magnifies every little circumstance, so you are continually making yourself unhappy when no real cause exists. When you feel yourself acting out in jealousy, you need to examine the reason for your jealous feelings.

BATTLING INSECURITY:

What causes fights and quarrels among you? Don't they come from your desires that battle within you? You want something but don't get it. You kill and covet, but you cannot have what you want. You quarrel and fight. You do not have, because you do not ask God." (James 4: 1-3)

Desire does not ensure possession. James is not describing the condition of any special community, but analyzing the result of coveting things belonging to others out of jealousy. Many people desire things belonging to their friends, yet think to obtain them by envy, war and suppression. Their aim is to live in great power and plenty, in voluptuousness and prosperity, and thus struggle for what belongs to their friends. They fight but do not succeed, because they have wrong motives.

'Don't mind the fellow who belittles you; he is only trying to cut you down to his size.'

When you are battling insecurity, another person's achievements may come across to you as a threat. For example, your colleague and friend gets a salary rise for putting in an extra hour on an important project, or just got promoted, married or graduated etc. Instead of being thrilled for them, you feel jealous. You take their achievement as a direct reflection on your circumstances.

DESTRUCTIVE JEALOUSY: Destructive jealousy is real. The emotional threat that is provoking the jealousy is real and can be backed up with external evidence. The way this jealousy plays out is the problem. When feeling a destructive jealousy, people and friends, usually lash out at the person or people who they assume to have caused them harm. It is an angry jealousy that is rooted in revenge. A jealous friend would always compare themselves to successful friends, who have done more and better work and who have accumulated more reward. They may have an ideal family, a noble wife or husband, superb children, a luxurious home, yet all these do not seem to count for very much with them.

Their gaze is so set upon what their friends do or have, that they don't seem to know how to appreciate their own circumstance and always accuse them for not working harder. Many friends miss the joy they might experience in life by keeping their eyes fixed on that what belongs to other people. No person can enjoy their own opportunities for happiness while being jealous of another's. We lose the joy of living by not cheerfully accepting the little pleasures that come to our way daily, but instead longing and wishing for what belongs to others.

'We underrate that which we do possess' (or is it the other way round?)

JEALOUSY IS DANGEROUS:

"Who is wise and understanding among you? Let him show it by his good life, by deeds done in the humility that comes from wisdom. But if you harbor bitter envy or jealous and selfish ambition in your heart, do not boast about or deny the truth. Such wisdom does not come down from heaven but is earthly, unspiritual, of the devil. For where you have envy and selfish ambition, there you find disorder and every evil practice" (James 3: 13-16)

Jealousy is dangerous and deadly, it is not an effective protection mechanism as long as its focus is on hurting and not finding a solution. Jealousy may even go as far to lead to murder. Wherever jealousy is, everything is unsettled and agitated. There is no mutual confidence; there is no unity of purpose, action, also, no co-operation in promoting a common objective and no stability in any plan. All love and harmony, of course, are banished, all happiness disappears and all prosperity comes to an end. In place of peaceful virtues, there springs up every evil passion that tends to mar the peace that should characterise friendship. Where the spirit of jealousy prevails in a friendship or a relationship, it is impossible to expect progress in both earthly and divine things, and in such friendship any effort towards self-development is vain.

"After a man makes his mark in the world, a lot of people will come around with an eraser." (Anonymous)

DEALING WITH JEALOUSY:

"We who are strong ought to bear with the failings of the weak and not to please ourselves. Each of us should please his neighbor or friend for his good, to build him up. Even Christ did not please Himself but, as it is written: The results of those who insult you have fallen on me."
(Romans 15: 1-3)

A friend who possesses the spirit of jealousy is weak, therefore needs your help. Often when you have a jealous friend it comes out in their behavior. You can usually pick it up in their verbal and body language. You can have a friend that you have been connected to for years that envies your accomplishments but still loves you. One thing you should always do is give out positive vibes and inspiration to your friends and never want them to think you are putting yourself on a higher level. Words of encouragement and detailed motivational advice can turn the jealousy into admiration. It is good to understand your friends in every situation, as with understanding you would be able to feel and view what led to the jealousy. Everyone has a problem, so it's good to disclose that your life also has its ups and downs. Never make your friend think you feel like you have a care-free life. Be realistic and mindful of his situation; never put yourself on a higher pedestal, stay down to earth. Just demonstrate the perspective of how to measure your problems in a positive and realistic way. Avoid all negative tendencies by identifying with their situation. You can not satisfy every need of your friend and you surely cannot change the way they are. But you can encourage and inspire them to strive towards a more productive and satisfying life.

A good friend will deny their own humor, in consideration of their friend's. Just as the Lord Jesus Christ accommodated his weak disciples, you must also bear the infirmities of the jealous spirit of your friend by showing empathy and sympathy, while, ministering strength and praying for them.

FRIENDSHIP AND SUSPICION:

"And Saul eyed David from that day forward." (1 Samuel 18: 9)

The Greek word 'eyed' is 'een hupoblepomeuos,' which means 'suspicion.' The above verse means that Saul suspected David. Proud men or so called friends cannot withstand praise of others rather than of themselves and expect every honor to be showered on them alone. Every relationship is anchored on trust, love, personalisation and fairness. But the moment you begin to suspect your spouse or friend, love, which is the basis of your relationship, disappears and troubles fueled by suspicion take its place. Close friends who give room to third party influence are prone to welcome negative ideas, which will definitely lead to suspicion. It often happens that the source of suspicion is the desire for revenge, malice and envy, and since we cannot take vengeance practically on our friends and/or express it verbally, we become judgmental and withdraw our friendship by recoiling into ourselves.

THE ROOT OF SUSPICION: Suspicion is cognition of mistrust in which a person doubts the honesty of another person or believes another person to be guilty of some wrongdoing or crime, but without sure proof. It is the tendency to doubt the trustworthiness of a relation or friend. The word comes from the Italian word **'sospetto,'** which means, **'to watch.'** English philosopher, statesman and author, Francis Bacon (1561-1626) advised that:

"**suspicions need to be repressed and well-guarded, because otherwise they will cloud the mind, and cause the ruler to move towards tyranny, due to the fear that his subjects are conspiring against him, and a husband to become jealous and fearful of his wife's interaction with other men.**"

The wisdom here is that friends who harbor suspicion should be frank with their friends concerning the subject of their suspicion in order to clear the air.

HISTORY OF SUSPICION:

"**Suspicion always haunts the guilty mind.**" **(William Shakespeare - English poet and playwright 1564-1616)**

"**Suspicion is black poison that infects the human mind like the plague.**" **(English dramatist, poet and actor 1572-1637)**

"**Suspicion is a useless pain in which a person has a belief that a formidable evil lies within all of his or her fellow men.**" **(Dr Samuel Johnson - English writer 1709-1784)**

"**Suspicion is like heavy armour that impedes humans more than it protects them.**" **(Robert Burns - Scottish Poet 1759-1796)**

It is clear to see the effects of suspicion have provoked many reactions none of which are very favourable from many noted writers down the years, including; Mahatma Gandhi who warned that if suspicions arise about any of a person's motives, then all of their acts can become tainted with this mistrust and uncertainty.

Suspicion causes misunderstanding between friends. It is the greatest hindrance to friendly co-operation as well as unity and solidarity of hearts, and leads a friend to an individualistic life, solitude and isolation. Suspicion does not let friends trust one another and causes friends to spy on each other. Many families and friendships have been broken up by suspicion, and a lot of competent and innocent men have been killed, just because of mistrust. Suspicion has ignited many great wars. Suspicion is no less an enemy to happiness. They that become suspicious will quickly become corrupt. Suspicion is the child of guilt. It is a vain and foolish pride, which would teach that everyone is conspiring against your happiness or has evil plans concerning your reputation and business. The fact is, probably no one is thinking of you. You are continually making yourself unhappy when no real cause exists. You are to fight against such an unfortunate disposition at all times, which can be eradicated.

THE SAD EFFECTS OF SUSPICION: Have you wondered why a climate of suspicion pervades and destroys so many relationships? It persists amongst men and women alike. Men are constantly on edge that once their women are out the doors they are after another man somewhere. Women also think their men are chasing some girl out there behind their backs. Once their partner's phone fails to ring, they must have switched off their handset to forestall any interruption of their pleasure spree or detection of their location. If the line rings at the other end but no answer, then something amiss is going on.

Ladies constantly search their men's shirt and trouser pockets with the anticipation of picking up something suspicious while men always scroll through their women's phonebooks and SMS directory checking for any strange numbers or text messages. Even funnier scenarios abound where ladies hug their men, sniffing them for any strange perfume and vice versa. Every new action, dress or fragrance is examined. This whole drama almost leaves the victim in a state of dilemma. Some serious-minded, loyal and sincere partners or friends have had to suffer in silence enduring and tolerating such unhealthy climate of suspicion. Once blissful relationships or friendships have been destroyed, and the foundations of several friendly unions have cracked, exposing great secrets.

DEFEATING SUSPICION: Why would two professed lovers or friends who have pledged commitment to each other's happiness turn around and begin to undermine the same happiness they have pledged to ensure? Francis Bacon (philosopher) argued that the root of suspicion is a lack of knowledge; as such the remedy to suspicion is to learn about the issue that is troubling you.

To defeat suspicion, you first have to understand the nature of the suspicious mind. The suspicious mind is suffering from deeply ingrained insecurities acquired during childhood, possibly due to an acute feeling of insecurity and fears acquired from over-controlling or an unloving relationship with parents or care givers. Hence, the suspecting mind is interpreting the world through the frame of the feeling of inadequacy, fear of loss, low self-image, a feeling of being unloved or insecurity. The suspicious personality is judging people by projecting their own insecurities on to them, hence, if they see the spouse or friend laughing or talking to someone, they feel threatened and their mind starts pointing accusing fingers and cries of cheating, even though it is their own feelings of low self-image, lack of confidence and fear of loss, that is making them interpret an honest every day event in such a manner.

Now, if you are a victim of a suspicious mind, that is, experiencing suspicion and accompanying harshness at the hand of someone else. Here are some ideas what to do:

1. **Work on developing trust with that person; explain your own feelings and actions to that person in detail.**
2. **Take them into confidence and tell them everything. Be transparent.**
3. **Open the channels of honest communication, and listen to that person's fears and feelings to help them view things differently.**
4. **Be sympathetic, understanding and appreciative of that person to gain their confidence.**
5. **Love and emotionally support that person as much as you can. If you really love them you can help them to overcome their deeply ingrained insecurities.**

If you are suffering from a suspicious mind yourself, here is a practice you have to follow to overcome suspicious tendencies: repeat the affirmation:

"I totally and completely love and accept myself. I believe in the Lord and myself. I forgive (add the name of the person you suspect.) in the name of Jesus. Amen."

Constantly depend on the word of God, prayer and fasting. Every person in this world has some or other issues in their life to deal with; it is not a shame to need to deal with and overcome issues you may have deeply ingrained in your mind. What is egoistic and shameful is not recognizing these issues, or not being ready to overcome them, even though, they may be destroying your life. It is your choice to decide whether you want to be right and live right.

FRIENDSHIP AND TRUST:

"Do not trust a neighbor; put no confidence in a friend. Even with her who lies in your embrace be careful of your words. For a son dishonors his father, a daughter shall rise up against her mother, a daughter-in-law against her mother-in-law. A man's enemies are the members of his own household." (Micah 7: 5-6)

"A man's enemy will be the members of his own household." (Matthew 1: 35-36)

Considering the modern world, human nature has changed very little. Society has crumbled at its roots; the enemies of a man are those of his own household. Suspicion, distrust, and enmity have become the norm. Thus, Micah the prophet in his days warned the people not to trust a friend, because there is no real trust in any. Micah's reason was that; men were betrayed by their households for private interests, or for revenge, because they would not join in things unlawful. John the beloved said; "believe not every spirit, but try the spirits, whether they are of God." Micah is asking us not to distrust all people, though cautioning us to be careful and to know who we call a friend, before trusting them with all our heart and the secrets of our lives.

WHAT IS TRUST: We all need friends; they help us make life worth living. They nurture, support, love, listen, and share life with us. Friendships are to be maintained; they do not just happen or continue on their own. A friend shows empathy, sympathy and understanding. Friends show real concern and allow you to share your thoughts and feelings without judgment. All of these attributes lead to a bonding and trust. Trust means assured resting of the mind of something or somebody. It is a situation in which you expose your vulnerabilities to people or friends, but believing they will not take advantage of your openness. It is to place your confidence in something, or your parents, siblings or a friend etc.

To trust a friend is to rely or depend on them in the cause of life's disappointments and victories. We talk of placing our trust in someone, which shows that it involves an action rather than just our feelings. Trust is the foundation on which friendship is built. Our ability to trust may be affected by our upbringing and/or past experiences. It is very easy within a friendship to assume we view trust in the same way as our friends, but assumptions can be misleading and lead to disappointment causing hurt, when things go wrong or when trust is not properly handled. Trust is the treasure of our daily lives. However, we do not understand its value. It is generally thought that trust in our daily lives is disappearing fast. Why have we become so suspicious, that we cannot enter into meaningful friendship with others?

Man was created to trust. The first lesson we learnt at our

birth was trust, as babies trust their mothers instinctively. As our lives progress, trust begins to diminish. Our childhood innocence gives way to calculations in which there is no place for trust. Trust in each other gives strength and vitality to our friendship. It gives us inner happiness, which is priceless. It brings joy around and life appears brighter and brighter. When you trust another you feel self- confident. Trust keeps friends in a positive framework. It not only provides a sense of security, but also provides us new zeal to fight the battles of life. Trusting each other gives us a sense of deep bonding. It means we are united to fight the battle ahead.

WHERE THERE IS NO TRUST: We behave mechanically to each other when there is no trust. Life appears to be devoid of colour and lacks spontaneity. We live in a suppressed condition, which inhibits the growth of our personality. As a result, we are not able to contribute towards the betterment of our friendship, which invariably affects our society. A friendship whose foundation is built on friendship is progressive and dynamic. Lack of trust signifies a setback in the friendship. When trust gets broken it can be difficult to deal with. It can leave you feeling betrayed, vulnerable, and confused. Trust is elementary to a good friendship and should not be taken for granted or ignored. The importance of trust is friendship; friendship is based on trust, and it is important because, it is what keeps the bond of the friendship going. If you do not trust someone, it is next to impossible to be friends. Your friends are the people you tell your secrets to, rely on and spend time with. If you do not trust in a friendship, you better stay out of it. If you want to stay in the friendship and remain a good friend, it is important to understand and apply the ins and outs of trust.

BUILDING TRUST: Building trust is not easy. A lot of conscious efforts have to be made in this direction. We need to nurture our friendship with care and should not let our ego destroy our relationship. This requires making constant efforts to know each other fully. Most of the problems in friendship occur because we do not want to open up; as a result we tend to look at others with doubt. No doubt people tend to view us with suspicion. Trust building must start with us. After all, reform begins at home. Let us reform ourselves by giving time to our friendship and thinking of ways to strengthen them. Trust will then follow naturally.

FRIENDS WHO OUTSTAY THEIR WELCOME:

"Let your foot seldom be in your neighbor's house, least he become tired of you and hate you." (Proverbs 25: 17)

The book of Proverbs is significant as to the relation of friend to friend, and how reciprocal love may be turned into hatred, by too much outstaying one's welcome. It is wisdom, as well as good manners, not to be troublesome to your friends with your visits, and not to visit too often, or stay too long. You should endeavour not to come at mealtime, or make yourself busy in the affairs of their families, as you thereby make yourself cheap, mean, and burdensome. 'Let him who seeks esteem come seldom.'
Do not make yourself common. Do not come at unreasonable times, or ask for help too often. Intrusiveness, and not intimacy, is to be shunned. 'Familiarity breeds contempt.' They that sponge upon their friends lose them!

Have you ever had guests at home that just didn't seem to want to leave? Many a time when you have a party or friends come for a mere visit or something, even if you only have a few friends over, some of them just don't seem to leave at the time you want them to. When this happens, come up with a list of things to do, to possibly alleviate the problem and get these people to leave, without being rude or disrespectful. 'Set Rules,' before anyone actually sets foot on your doorstep, make sure you are clear as to how long you are expecting them to stay. Set your availability in advance, let everyone be clear with the time you have and want to share.

THE PERFECT GUEST:

"Do not be afraid. I bring you good news of great joy that will be for all the people." (Luke 2: 10)

Here is the picture of a perfect guest. The angel came as a guest from heaven, who visited Mary with a matter of great joy. The angel came with a message of blessing. Mary was terrified by his appearance but, he encouraged her not to be afraid, for he had come not to harm, but to bless her.
This perfect guest did not come to declare a curse, but the Lord's merciful loving-kindness, the subject being a matter of great joy. What a great lesson to learn, that guests should be carriers of great and good news into the homes of their friends. Do you want to be invited back after a visit? Honour your invitation if you can, if not, inform the host about your unavailability. Be punctual with your appointments, don't be early, and don't be late. The successful man in every calling has had a keen sense of the value of time.

"The man who is good at excuses is good for nothing else."

You have every right to waste your own time, <u>but not</u> other peoples, by your lack of punctuality.

Never visit with an empty hand. Bring something with you, a small gift e.g. flowers, chocolates, toffees or something the host can enjoy later. Don't sit back and wait to be entertained. Take part in the conversation, but don't hog it. Don't overstay your welcome! You don't want your friend, the host, to sit there thinking, please leave I need to sleep. Don't leave by just wandering off, seek out your host, thank them for a lovely time and then go. You may later again, say thank you by e-mail, a phone or a note, they will always value it.

CHAPTER 8

FRIENDSHIP AND ARGUMENT

"By pride comes nothing but argument, but with the well-advised is wisdom." (Proverbs 13: 10)

"Then there was a sharp contention (argument), and they separated. And so Barnabas chose Mark and sailed to Cyprus; but Paul chose Silas and departed." (Acts 15: 39)

Argument, simply means to reason to support or contest an opinion. To dispute or quarrel, or to contend or maintain, as by giving reasons. The issue of the above referenced argument and disagreement, is that Barnabas was peremptory that he would not go with Paul, unless they took John Mark with them; Paul was peremptory that he would not go if John Mark was to go with them. Neither would yield nor submit, therefore, there was no other remedy than for them to separate and part Company. The best of friends are but frail men, subject to faults, as the two good men had expressly demonstrated. Paul would not trust John Mark. The affection of Barnabas led him to hope for the best, and was therefore, desirous to give John Mark the benefit of doubt and a second chance. Barnabas would not give up, Paul would not agree, therefore, they agreed to depart from each other.

"Be careful what you say, friendship can end in one minute because of a stupid word." (Anonymous-but wise person)

WHY DO FRIENDS ARGUE? Friends can argue about a variety of things, where to hang out, who to hang out with, maybe about, what one of them said, what one of them did, and so on.

Disagreements, misrepresentations and misunderstandings, are very common between friends. So, what should you do when you get into an argument with a friend? First, ask yourself if the problem is worth arguing about. Most of the time, friends argue over little things that don't really matter. Once you realise how worthless the argument is, it will be wise to call a truce, and to compromise, then forget about it.

"The more arguments you win, the fewer friends you will have" **(Sophocles-Greek tragedian playwright circa. 497 BC)**

The truth is friends argue because they care about each other. They care about each other's ideas, opinions, and desires. So, when they disagree, they are likely to try to change the other's mind, because they really want to agree with each other, and it hurts when they don't agree. Unfortunately, it also hurts when they argue, so they really need to follow the advice given above.

"Truth springs from arguments amongst friends." **(David Hume-** *Scottish philosopher 1711-1776)*

FRIENDSHIP AND CRITICISM:

"Then Miriam and Aaron spoke against Moses because of the Cushite woman he had married; and they said, 'Has the Lord indeed spoken only through Moses? Has He not spoken through us as well?' and the Lord heard it."
(Numbers 12: 1-2)

Criticism is the act of examining and judging severely. It also means severe or unfavorable judgment. Criticism of others is a sin! It is a sin we find easy to excuse in ourselves if we label it as 'constructive criticism,' how often have you either heard or used this adage? Your so-called constructive criticism is very often *'constrictive criticism.'* Rather than encouraging and helping our friends, we stifle their personalities and stunt their growth by our *'constrictive' comments.* Moses was criticized by his brother, Aaron, and his sister, Miriam. Miriam and Aaron criticized Moses on two grounds; his marriage and his ministry, as God's leading spokesman. Although they had significant positions, they were still jealous of the fact that he had an unfair monopoly on revelations from God. The beautiful lesson here is that, Moses was not offended by their criticism.

"Never worry about the criticism from the misinformed."
(Adolph Rupp - famous American basketball coach 1901-1977)

All criticism is not bad. God forbid that we should turn a deaf ear to our friends who disagree with us.

"Faithful are the wounds of a friend." (Proverbs 27: 6)

Who's Your Friend?

Some friends are in our lives to save us from ourselves. As believers, the trick is to create an environment that is safe for dissension, so our friends can speak up.

DESTRUCTIVE CRITICISM:

(This is a copy of the letter they sent him.)

To King Artaxerxes,

From your servants in Trans-Euphrates:

The king should know that the people who came up to us from you have gone to Jerusalem and are rebuilding that rebellious and wicked city. They are restoring the walls and repairing the foundations.

Furthermore, the king should know that if this city is built and its walls are restored, no more taxes, tribute or duty will be paid, and eventually the royal revenues will suffer. Now since we are under obligation to the palace and it is not proper for us to see the king dishonored, we are sending this message to inform the king, so that a search may be made in the archives of your predeces-sors. In these records you will find that this city is a re-bellious city, troublesome to kings and provinces, a place with a long history of sedition. That is why this city was destroyed. We inform the king that if this city is built and its walls are restored, you will be left with nothing in Trans-Euphrates. *(Ezra 4: 11-16)*

The general purport of the letter was to destructively criticize the Jews before the king. Destructive criticism means criticizing and pointing out mistakes, without taking the time to suggest ways of improvement. It is degrading; it shoots down somebody's work unnecessary, and unless you are willing to show that friend a constructive way to improve, you really have no right to point out mistakes of your friends. Destructive criticism attempts to deflect the attention from the real issue, which might be something as basic as jealousy. Destructive criticism comes from the heart where love is lacking, at least in that moment. Love is the antidote for destructive criticism. Destructive criticism is motivated by fear, a fear of being discovered, or of being criticized and having to be open and honest. When you are motivated by love, you are less likely to be critical of others, because you will have their best interests in mind.

*"There will be a time when loud-mouthed, incompetent people seem to be getting the best of you. When that happens, you only have to be patient and wait for them to self destruct. It never fails." (*Richard Rybolt-author)

CONSTRUCTIVE CRITICISM:

"When Jethro saw everything that Moses had to do, he asked, 'what is all this that you are doing for the people? Why are you doing this all alone, with the people standing here from morning till night to consult you?' Then Jethro said, 'You are not doing it the right way. You will wear out yourself out and these people as well. Now let me give you some good advice, and God will be with you.' Moses took Jethro's advice and those capable men from among all the Israelites." (Exodus 18: 14-20)

Here is a great prudence and consideration of Jethro as a friend. He disliked the method Moses used, and was so free with him to criticize. Moses did not despise this criticism, because he saw and heard God in it.

"To avoid criticism do nothing, say nothing, be nothing."
*(*__Elbert Hubbard-American writer and philosopher 1856-1915__*)*

From this example, we can see that constructive criticism entails telling people how to improve than simply shooting their work down, rather than saying that everything is wrong. To constructively criticize a friend, means to make sure that you are knowledgeable enough, or dedicated enough to be positive and not just point out mistakes, but suggest ways to improve on those mistakes. Otherwise, what good is your comment? Without the constructive basis for the critique, all you have done is either deliberately or unwittingly, belittled your friend's work. If you want to point out something that you think is wrong, explain why you think it is wrong, then, give your suggestion for correcting or improving future works.

"Keep away from people who try to belittle your ambition. Small people always do that, but the really great make you feel that you, too, can become great."
(Samuel Langhorne Clemens, better known as 'Mark Twain' - American author and humorist 1835-1910)

FRIENDSHIP AND ADVICE:

The way of a fool is right in his own eyes, but he who heeds

advice is wise. (Proverbs 12: 15)
Listen to advice and receive instruction, that you may be wise in your latter days. (Proverbs 19: 20)
Confess your faults one to another and pray for one another. (James 5: 16)

'Advice' is a suggestion to a person about what they should do. It is an opinion, direction, guidance or help, about what could or should be done about a situation or problem. It is well with friends that are wise in their latter end, and for the future state. Friends that are wise in their endeavors must hear counsel or receive instruction, they must be willing to be taught and ruled, willing to be advised and corrected. What is it that keeps a friend from being wise; he thinks he is right in everything he does, and therefore asks no advice, because he does not think he needs it, he is confident that he knows the way, and cannot miss it, therefore, never enquires for advice. The rule he goes by is to do that which is right in his own eyes, to walk in the way of his heart. *'Quicquid libet, licet' (He makes his will his law).*

He is not wise that is governed by his eyes and not by his conscience. It is what keeps him from being a fool, if he is willing to be advised by his wise and good friends. He desires to have counsel given him and being corrected in his judgment and having a value for the direction of his friends.

CAUTION WHEN TAKING ADVICE: Anyone can give advice, but some people do so only in their own interest. Be careful when somebody offers you a piece of advice. Find out first what their interest in the matter is, because, you can be sure that they are thinking primarily of themselves. Why should he come out on top instead of you? He will assure you that things look good, and then stand back to watch what happens to you. Don't ask advice of a friend whom you don't trust, and don't give advice to a friend who is jealous of you. Don't ask for advice about an enemy of his, or ask a coward friend for advice about war, a merchant about a bargain, a buyer about selling, a stingy friend about gratitude, a cruel friend about kindness, a casual worker about finishing a job, or a lazy friend about a difficult task. Pay no attention to any advice they may give. Instead, rely on a friend who is positive in both the spiritual and physical endeavors of life. Above all, pray to God that he will direct you to the right place, to the right person at the right time.

GIVING ADVICE CAN BE DANGEROUS: Your advice to a best friend may be well being helpful, but if it means that your best friend must put in some work and effort, he will like to discard it. Giving advice may not be a waste of your time and energy, but it can be dangerous to your friendship. It is particularly dangerous to offer advice when you haven't been asked for it, or when it involves the truth. It is best to avoid getting involved in people's personal affairs, especially, if you haven't been asked. Trying to solve their problem is to say they are not capable of doing it on their own.

"Wise men don't need advice. Fools don't take it."
(Benjamin Franklin 1706-1790 - American author and a Founding Father of the USA)

The problem is, the advice we give friends may be the opposite of what they expect or desire.

"When a man comes to me for advice, I find out the kind of advice he wants, and I give it to him" (Josh Billings 1818-1885 - *American humorist*)

Whenever you feel compelled to respond to a request for advice, say it simply, make it short, don't rant and rave and be sensitive.

"Whatever your advice (to a best friend), make it brief."
(Horace 65-8 BC - leading Roman lyric poet)

CHAPTER 9

OVERCOMING REJECTION

"He has removed my brothers far from me, and my acquaintances are completely estranged from me. My relatives have failed, and my close friends have forgotten me. Those who dwell in my house, and my maidservants, count me as a stranger; I am like a foreigner before them. I call my servant, but he gives no answer; I beg him with my mouth. My breath is offensive to my wife, and I am repulsive to the children of my own body. Even young children reject me; I arise, and they speak against me. All my close friends reject me, and those whom I love have turned against me. Have pity on me, have pity on me, O you my friends." (Job 19: 13-20)

What an accurate description of rejection this biblical passage describes!

In prosperity a man will be surrounded by his friends, but as soon as his prosperity is stripped away, and he is overwhelmed with trouble, they withdraw and reject him to suffer alone. Here, Job takes notice of the rejection and unkindness of his relations, who were bound by all the laws of friendship and civility to concern themselves for him, to visit him, enquire after him, and be ready to do him the good things that lay in their power.

They took no more care of him although he was a stranger whom they never knew. His kinsfolk, who claimed relation when he was in prosperity, failed him; they came short of their former friendship to him and his present expectation of kindness from them. Even his familiar friends, whom he was mindful of, had forgotten him, forgotten both his former friendliness to them and his present problems. Poor Job was misused and abused by his own family and some of his worst enemies were those of his own circle. Job, who was the master of his family ordinarily, expected to be attended to and taken care of by them, but he was totally rejected. Even his servants never heeded to his beck and call. Children, who were born in his house, never feared nor loved him.

Uncertain is the friendship of men, but if God be our friend, He will not fail us in time of need. But let none that pretend to humanity ever use their friends as Job's friends used and rejected him; adversity is the proof of friendship.

WHAT IS REAL REJECTION: Reject or rejection means refusal to accept, recognize, and believe, to cast away as worthless or discard. Rejection is an emotional, mental, and physically painful experience. In life, you are likely to experience an uncountable number of rejections. The people you are attracted to will not like you, jobs you want will be denied you, invitations you make will be declined, and things you produce will be snubbed. Whether you like it or not, this is inevitable.

Why is rejection so painful? When other people disapprove, disrespect or ignore us, it feels horrible. Anger, depression, and deep hurt can be the result. The reason is simple, in times past being rejected by our peers most likely meant death. Sometimes people get rejected for good reasons and sometimes they get rejected for bad reasons, but, either way, rejection hurts.

Some people are extraordinarily sensitive to rejection, even with minor things, which can send them into a state of extreme anger and frustration. Some react with levels of hostility and aggression that go far beyond reason.

"Don't let anyone, or any rejection, keep you from what you want." (Ashley Tisdae - American actress and singer)

DEALING WITH REJECTION:

"Let no man despise your youth, but be an example to the believers in word, in conduct, in love, in spirit, in faith, (1 TIimothy 4: 19) *in purity."*

To be despised or rejected is to be regarded as worthless, to look down on someone. Paul tells Timothy that the antidote to rejection is holding on to oneself. He asked him not to act in such a manner that any should reject or look down on account of his present condition. In our rejection we must behave ourselves with gravity and prudence, which might gain respect.

"There's nothing like rejection to make you do an inventory of yourself." (James Lee Burke - *American author*)

There are people who avoid rejection at all cost and never take any risk or put themselves in a situation where they could be rejected. On the other hand there are people who do not let rejection stop them from trying again. One of the best signs of a mature person is how they react when they are despised or rejection. It is very important when dealing with rejection to first acknowledge it to yourself, then to people close to you. Do not tell the world, but it is good to talk about it with those you trust. Pick yourself up and move on with your life. Have confidence in God and in yourself. I mean, if God is with you, who can be against you? Do not give up or quit whatever you desire or aspire to be, try, try and try again.

"Rejection is nothing more than a necessary step in the pursuit of success." **(Bo Bennet - American entrepreneur and business man)**

DEALING WITH PEOPLE WHO DRAG US DOWN:

"Do not repay anyone evil for evil. Be careful to do what is right in the eyes of everybody. If it is possible, as far as it depends on you, live at peace with everyone. Do not take revenge, my friends, but leave room for God wrath, for it is written: "It is mine to avenge; I will repay," says the Lord. "If your enemy is hungry, feed him; if he is thirsty, give him something to drink. in doing this, you will heap burning coals on his head." do not overcome by evil, but overcome evil with good." *(Romans 12: 17-21)*

We should always strive not to begin or originate a quarrel, but to seek and make peace. However, it does not always depend on us, as others may oppose and persecute us, or may start an assault on our personality or property. For their insults, persecution, hatred, ridicule or evil speaking we are not answerable, but we are answerable for our conduct towards them.

It may not be possible to prevent their injuring us, but it is possible not to begin a fight or quarrel with them. It always takes two to argue! We are called to be harmless and offensive, not giving others the occasion to quarrel with us. We are to remain uneventful, demonstrating the wisdom from above, which is pure and peaceable. It takes all kinds of people to make up the world we live in, and in life, we have the opportunity to meet many people. Although, some of them we may find are too difficult to deal with. These are the people we end up disliking, and we try and avoid them as much as possible. Keeping well away from them might be the right thing to do, but sometimes there are situations where it is impossible to avoid them. Happy and friendly people have the ability to uplift others who may be rejected or offended. However, when dealing with difficult people it is important to distinguish between what is right and responsible. Under certain circumstances, we feel obliged to adapt and agree with them, but we need to be careful we do not give up our rights at the same time.

DO NOT RETALIATE: Retaliation means to fight back or repay an injury, wrong or damage. The important thing to remember is that we do not retaliate in the same way as the person is treating us. Treat them with respect at all times and learn to listen to them, allowing them to air their point of view even after they have offended us. This will enable us to understand them better. Often it is also the case that once we get to know a person whom we thought was difficult we are able to deal with them easier.

It is important to remember that difficult people are most often the ones that have real issues in their lives. Take away the problem from the person, and try and see that person as an individual. After all, provided this person does not overstep their boundaries, they will eventually see that we also deserve respect. We are unable to change other people, but can of course influence and stop ourselves from becoming affected, therefore, demonstrating a good example. We need to accept that when dealing with people who bring us down, we cannot change them, but our actions coupled with the word of God can, bearing in mind we may also need to change certain things about ourselves. By changing our own perception, we may be able to deal with a situation more effectively. It is always easier to look into ourselves first and try and make internal changes. After all we all have our issues, don't we?

CONSTRUCTION AND INFLUENCE: If the other person is willing to make adjustments, then we need to influence them constructively. It is better to be tactful when sending a message, so the other person does not end up feeling worse. Some people influence our lives very badly, but we can be a positive influence on other people's lives by letting go of what we cannot control and doing our best to be helpful instead.

"We must be the change we want to see in the world. In the same way let us serve as inspiration to many and be the positive influence. If we do this we will find ourselves surrounded only by people we like and respect." (**Mahatma Gandhi 1869-1948 - prominent leader of Indian Nationalism**)

OVERCOMING LONELINESS:

"People who do not get along with others are interested only in themselves; they will disagree with what everyone else knows is right." (Proverbs 18: 1)

He who separates himself can make little progress in the investigation of divine and natural things. This person is in the center of his own existence, has a wife or husband, maybe a child or children, or a legal heir or friend, yet is as intent on getting money as if he had the largest family to provide for. This person stands alone in the world, without object for his variance, and without a friend to break his dreary isolation. Loneliness is living in seclusion and often having a lack of friendship. Society is the balm of life. For anyone to be entirely excluded from all human intercourse, would make a person isolated and miserable. Men and women were formed for society and not made solely for themselves; they are also not capable of living in the world totally independent of others. The wants and weaknesses of mankind render society necessary for their convenience, safety and support.

THE PAIN OF LONELINESS: Loneliness is one of the major problems facing mankind today. It is amazing with a world population of almost seven billion people, that some people can still feel all alone. Once Adam's relationship with God was disrupted, humanity suffered the pain of feeling lonely. Loneliness is best defined as; 'an emotional feeling of being sad and dejected because of a lack of companionship from others.' Loneliness can result in sick feelings of being left out of the crowd, or unwanted. Some lonely people feel cut off from the rest and have an extreme lack of meaningful contact with other people. They have an intense longing to be needed and wanted by someone else. Some people suffer from loneliness only from time to time, and for some it is a daily way of life. Most lonely people wear the effects of it on their face with a sad and dejected look.

"The most terrible poverty is loneliness and the feeling of being unloved" (Agnes Gonxha Bojaxhiu 1910-1997 'Mother Teresa')

In advanced stages of loneliness some people attempt to escape it through alcohol, drugs, or other diversions. Loneliness can periodically afflict anyone, it plays no favorites. Many great men of the bible spoke of being alone and feeling the pain of loneliness on several occasions.

I lie awake; I have become like a bird alone on a roof. (Psalm 102: 7)

CAUSES OF LONELINESS: In today's society, because many people do not have time for close relationships they tend to isolate themselves and have no meaningful contact with others. Other people harbour several different negative attitudes that create loneliness in their lives. Things like self-pity, which serve to nurse a constant self-doubt and self-critical image that nobody cares for them. If negative attitudes like self-pity, self-centeredness, anger, fear can reinforce loneliness, the best and only thing to do is to stay away from them. Fear can raise its head in many forms, e.g. rejection, intimidation, lack of intimacy, and the fear of being hurt, are allowed to persist in someone's life.

A cycle of loneliness will deepen into the person's soul and this will make it impossible to fellowship with others. Also, there are circumstances that happen in the lives of people from time to time that can create feelings of loneliness. When we face situations like grieving over the death of a spouse or loved one, divorce, or being single, we can be susceptible to loneliness. Other situations like being wealthy, exceptionally talented, handicapped, or maybe a newcomer to an area, all these can create loneliness in our lives.

"It is so lonely when you even don't know yourself."
(Anonymous)

THE REMEDY FOR LONELINESS: Loneliness does not have to be a dead end for you. God understands your feelings, for He Himself has suffered the same feelings when through his incarnate self on this earth in the form of His Son, Jesus Christ;

"Eli, Eli, lama sabachthani?" meaning, *"My God, My God, why have you forsaken Me?" (Matthew 27: 46)*

The spirit of life is society, which of society is freedom and that of freedom is the discreet and modest use of it. You cannot alleviate loneliness until you deal with the root cause of the loneliness. You must openly deny negative traits that are alienating you from others. You must take the initiative of reaching out to others. Smiles are free, handshakes are free, and listening carefully cost nothing. Firstly, be nice to people and eventually others will reciprocate. Decide to be friendly and co-operative, 'make love not war' with the people who come along in life. Join a group in an area where you do not have to compete and just relax. Forget about winning and try liking, blessing and being friendly. Relationships do not just happen; you must invest your time and effort in order to develop them. Make allies, form networks, make relationships part of your lifestyle. There is an old saying:

'He travels faster who travels alone, but it is also true that "he travels farthest who travels with friends' (Anonymous)

The question still remains, who is your friend?

FRIENDSHIP AND HAVING SELF CONTROL:

"Better a patient man than a warrior, a man who controls his temper than who takes a city" (Proverbs 16: 32).

War is harder when waged with one's own passion than one which is waged against others. He who conquers him or herself is of good use to them, and injures nobody; he that is slow to anger overcomes himself, and by himself; he overcomes not only men, but also the rulers of darkness of this world. Who is a hero? A hero simply conquers his desire.

"Break your head, not so sore; break your will –that is more" **(Matthew Claudius*.)*

It is only victory that does no harm, no lives or treasures are sacrificed when it is concerned. Self-control is to have dominion over our spirit, appetites, affection, and all inclinations, but particularly, our passions and keeping them under absolute check and balance. There have been many great men and women, who had conquered nations, and yet were slaves to their own desires or passions. There have been great men and women who have lost their friends because they were slaves to uncontrolled anger and destroyed their best and most intimate of friendships. Who is really your friend?

CONTROL YOUR WORDS: It is necessary for one to be happy and exercise control over your words, as well as your actions, for there are words that strike even harder than blow from a sword through the heart. It says in the bible that words are like flaming arrows:

'They sharpen their tongues like swords and aim cruel words like deadly arrows.' (Psalm 64:3)

Character shows itself in control of speech as much as in anything else. The wise and forbearing friend will hold back their desire to say a smart or hard thing at the expense of another's feelings, while the unwise speak out what they think, and will sacrifice their friendship rather than their joke or comment.

There are friends who are headlong in their language as in their action because of lack of patience.

"I think the first virtue is to hold back the tongue: he approaches nearest to God, who knows how to be silent, even though he is in the right."(Marcus Porcius Cato 234-149 BC - Roman Statesman)

The state or nation that has the best government progresses most, so does the friend who governs the best in them self. No person is free who has not got control or command over them self, but allows their appetites or temper to control them. Many people often mistake strong feelings for strong character. A friend is not strong if they bear all before them, who frown on friendship and tremble on the contrary, they are weak. You must measure the strength of your friend by the power of the feelings by which they overcome obstacles, not by the power of those that overcome them. A friend who with strong passion remains disciplined, and face many provocations, yet hold them self and forgives; these are considerate and strong friends. Who is your friend?

CONTROL YOUR TEMPER:

"A quick-tempered man does foolish things, and a crafty man is hated." (Proverbs 14: 17)

A friend, who gets angry at any little thing, does foolish things. This proverb warns of human anger and its result in relation to others. Notice that two men are identified in the verse, along with their different characteristics, and are then noted in respect of their actions concerning those around them. A friend who is short tempered is also described as one who has a hasty spirit. A short-tempered friend, by his quick temper, does things that are senseless and morally wrong, therefore, no man desires his friendship. An intemperate friend will say and do what is ridiculous just like what Cain did to Able, *for example.* An uncontrolled friend has no time for reflection; he is hurried on by his passion; speaks without consideration, and acts without care.

"If you are intemperate, the chances are you might be in the wrong." (Anonymous)

A strong temper is not necessarily a bad temper. But the stronger the temper the greater is the need for self-discipline and self-control. Strong temper may only mean strong and influential will. Some of the greatest men and women in history have been men of strong tempers, but with great strength and determination to hold their will under strict regulation and control. A classic biblical example of temper and strength was Moses, his temper in the end cost him passing into Canaan, the Promised Land, although God did reward him and showed it to him, before handing over leadership to Joshua. **(See: Exodus 17 and Deutronomy 34)**

"Keep cool and you command everybody." **(St. Justin circa 100-165AD – Martyr)**

You can only control yourself if you desire to do so. The only way to control your friendship is have control over your temper. Controlling your temper is controlling your feelings, appetite, lust, and passion. We sin by excess of anger, lust, appetite, affection, love of authority, or praise. Few, if any are the sins that grow out to destroy our friendship.

TOO MUCH OF A GOOD THING IS NOT ALWAYS GOOD: A thing that is good is often only good as long as it is necessary, appreciated and respected. All things beyond necessity or what is necessary are often evil. For example, money is good and a necessity, but too much often leads to the love of it, which is evil. Light is also good but too much will blind you. Water is not only good but a real necessity, but too much can kill you by drowning. The same principle applies to heat as too much will burn us.

For the love of money is a root of all kinds of evil. Some people, eager for money, have wandered from the faith and pierced themselves with many griefs. *(1 Timothy 6:10)*

Praising people is good, but too much often can make people become proud and arrogant. It is essential to love life, but again too much can make you wretchedly unhappy. There are countless examples that can be offered but it is important to know that balance and perspective are very important. All species of intemperance grow from lack of self-control. To be a moderate friend one must master himself, must be brave, a noble fighter of every enemy within his own self. Man is born for dominion, but he must enter it by lawful conquest. If we are going to possess true friendship, we are to fight a bitter warfare against irritability, nervousness, jealousy, and all unkindness of heart and soul. We must be faithful to ourselves, faithful in our watch and have control over heart, tongue, eye, and hand. It is only by so doing that friendship can be maintained.

FRIENDSHIP AND ANGER:

"Do not make friends with a hot-tempered man. Do not associate with one easily angered, or you may learn his ways and get yourself ensnared." (Proverbs 22: 24-25)

Here is a warning against being a friend with an angry man. It is the law of friendship that we accommodate ourselves to our friends and be ready to serve them. Therefore, we should endeavour to be wise in the choice of friends we make. Though we must be friends to all, yet we must be careful whom we lay in our heart and contract familiarity with. Those we go with, we are apt to grow like.

Solomon's advice in the above scripture, when adhered can save us a lot of trouble and heartache. Why is this so? We have discovered that an angry person is known for the foolishness of his ways. When a person is controlled by anger his judgment is clouded. The result is a loss of the sense of purpose, and their actions are often out of proportion. Angry people cause trouble because they are quick to take offense and slow to forgive. Trying to help an angry person is an exercise in frustration. Such persons never seem to learn any lesson from the problems and bailing them out of trouble is counterproductive, because they begin to think they got away with something. The end result is that things get worse not better, so we are warned not to make friends with an angry person.

"Do not be misled: Bad company corrupts good character." (1 Corinthians 15: 33)

There is danger in having hot-tempered friends, as bad company and conversation are likely to make bad friendship. Those who would keep their innocence must keep good and meek company. Anger and vice are infectious, if we would avoid the contagion, we must keep clear of those who have it.

"He who walks with the wise grows wise, but a companion of fools suffers harm." (Proverbs 13: 20)

To walk in life with a person implies love and attachment, and if possible we imitate those we love. So we say:

"Show me his company, and I will tell you the man," let me know the company he keeps, and I shall easily guess his moral character.

FRIENDSHIP AND KINDNESS:

"Be kind and compassionate to one another, forgiving each other, just as in Christ God forgave you"
(Ephesians 4: 32)

The secret of true friendship is kindness or a desire to make another happy, and a true friend should be this kind of person. There is a hallow- hearted kindness, indeed, which is the true desire of a friend not to maim or copy.
A friend's politeness is based on kindness and their courtesy is the result of love, goodwill, and the happiness of others. A friend should have a heart disposed to empathy and compassion, and especially disposed to show kindness to the faults of erring friends. God has shown himself as kind and tenderhearted, and as we were created in Gods own image, meaning character, we therefore, in turn must show kindness to our fellow human beings, no matter what their shortcomings!

"Kindness never puts any person to needless pain."
*(***Anonymous***)*

Kindness is the music of good will to all men and is one of the purest traits of a heart of friendship. It guides friends wherever they may go and the never cease. To show kindness, it is not necessary to give large sums of money, or to perform wonderful actions that will lift up your name. It is simply, words of sympathy, giving a cup of cold water or food to the hungry, or discouraged and needy friends. Kindness does not consist in the gifts, but in gentleness and generosity of the spirit. Kindness is a feeling, of which no friend should be ashamed. Some friends may give their money, which comes from their purse, and hold back their kindness, which comes from their hearts. The kindness, which displays itself in giving money, does not amount to much, but the kindness of true sympathy. A true friend with true kindness will cherish and promote his friendship with practical good works. Little kindnesses shown are great ones. They drive away sadness, and cheer up the friendship.

Each of you should give what you have decided in your heart to give, not reluctantly or under compulsion, for God loves a cheerful giver. (2 Corinthians 9: 7)

THE LITTLE THINGS MATTER: Friendships are made up, not of great sacrifices or duties, but the little things, in which smiles and kindness given constantly are what wins and nurtures friendship. Kind efforts are not lost. Some may fall on good ground, and grow up into being 'charitable' in the mind of your friend. The noblest revenge you can take upon your enemies is to do them kindness. The tongue of a friend poised with kindness is full of pity, love and comfort. He speaks a word of comfort to a depressed friend, a word of sympathy to a bereaved friend, a word of encouragement to a stressed and sad friend, or a word of consolation to a dying friend. A true friend will not save his kind words and pleasing acts for they are great gifts, whose power will make those who receive them, happy in life. Speaking kindly to a friend lightens all the cares of the day and makes other affairs move along more smoothly in the friendship. Always leave home with kind words. They are jewels beyond price and powerful to heal the wounded hearts of your dear ones.

"When you are good to others, you are best to yourself."
(Anonymous)

FRIENDSHIP AND ETHICS:

"Do to others as you would have them do to you." (Luke 6: 31)

The Lord Jesus Christ commands us to do to others as we would like them to do to us. True friends must render all their due, and be honest and true in all their dealings. What they should expect, in reasonable terms, is to receive from their friends in justice or charity, and give the same. Ethics are the basic principles of right action or the standard of character set up by any race or nation. Jesus spoke these words as a positive rule for Christian living. What you do not want done to you, do not do to others. You reap what you sow!

Men have been preaching the 'Golden rule'as a suitable rule of conduct among men, but unfortunately the world accepts the letter, while totally missing the spirit behind this great statement.

"Unjust dealings always come home to roost."
(Anonymous)

"Whatsoever a friend sows that shall he also reap," it is your privilege to deal 'unfaithfully' with your friends, but, if you understand the law upon which the Golden Rule is based, you must know that your unfaithful dealing will come home to settle with you. A Friend, who understands the ethics of friendship would not strike back, but be kind to those who do him injustice. A friend, who believes in ethics, will understand that all human beings are bound in a single bond of fellowship and render it impossible for him to destroy another person by thought or action, without destroying himself. Understand the friendship ethics, and you will know that you are constantly punishing yourself for every wrong you do to your friends. A renowned author recommends that anyone one who wishes to follow the Golden Rule might follow these ethics:

- I believe in the Golden Rule as the basis of all human conduct; therefore, I will never do to My Friends that which I would not be willing for that person (My Friend) to do to me if our positions were reversed.
- I will be honest even in the slightest details, in all my transactions with My Friends, not because of my desire to be fair with them, but because of my desire to impress the idea of honesty on my subconscious mind, thereby weaving this essential quality into my own character.
- I will forgive my friends who are unfaithful toward me, with no thought as to whether they deserve it or not, because I understand the law through which forgiveness of others strengthen my own character and wipes out the effects of my own unfaithfulness in my mind.
- I will be faithful, generous, and fair with my friends always, even though I know that these acts will go unnoticed and unrewarded now.
- Whatever time I may spend to the discovery and exposure of the weakness and faults of my friends I will devote, more profitably to the discovery and

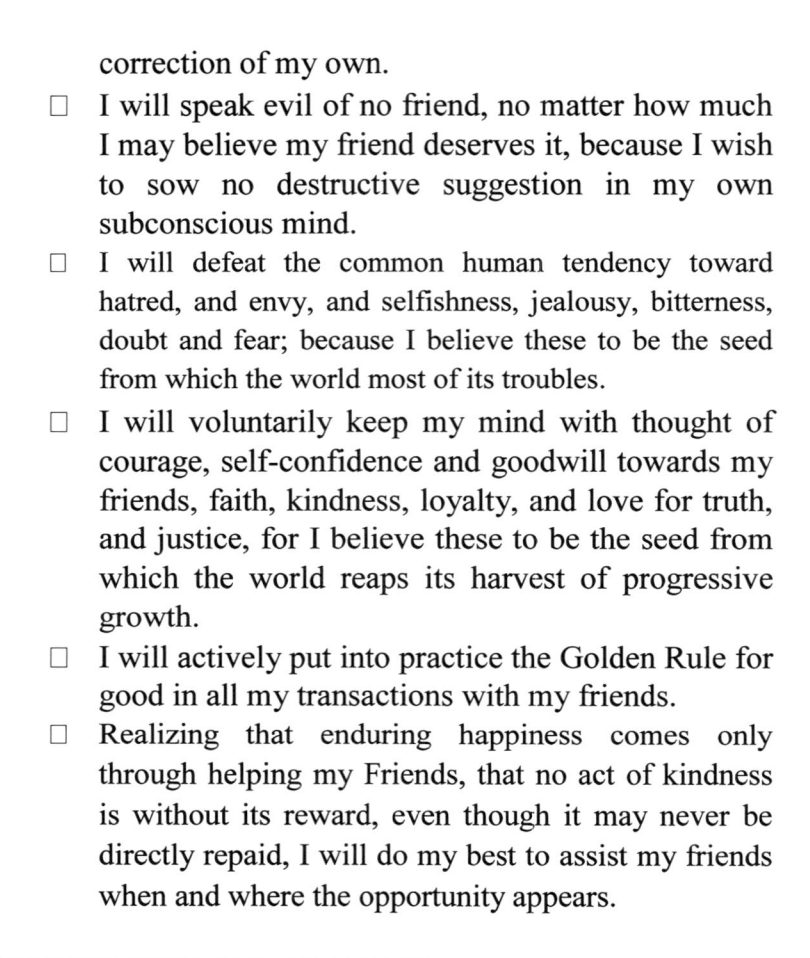

correction of my own.
- ☐ I will speak evil of no friend, no matter how much I may believe my friend deserves it, because I wish to sow no destructive suggestion in my own subconscious mind.
- ☐ I will defeat the common human tendency toward hatred, and envy, and selfishness, jealousy, bitterness, doubt and fear; because I believe these to be the seed from which the world most of its troubles.
- ☐ I will voluntarily keep my mind with thought of courage, self-confidence and goodwill towards my friends, faith, kindness, loyalty, and love for truth, and justice, for I believe these to be the seed from which the world reaps its harvest of progressive growth.
- ☐ I will actively put into practice the Golden Rule for good in all my transactions with my friends.
- ☐ Realizing that enduring happiness comes only through helping my Friends, that no act of kindness is without its reward, even though it may never be directly repaid, I will do my best to assist my friends when and where the opportunity appears.

FRIENDSHIP AND HEALTH:

"A wicked messenger falls into trouble, but a faithful ambassador brings health." (Proverbs 13: 17)

An ambassador, who faithfully discharges his duty, and serves the interest of those who employ him, is healthy. He is health to those by whom and for whom he is employed, so is a faithful friend, healing differences between them and keeps a good understanding, therefore, he is health to himself, for he secures his own interest.

The wicked and false friend inflicts pain on others and themselves, but faithful friends will find sound words to be healing others and themselves.

TWO ARE STRONGER THAN ONE: The conventional wisdom is that good friendship enhances an individual's sense of happiness and overall well- being. Also, a number of studies support the notion that strong social support improves a woman's prospect for good health and longevity. It has been shown that loneliness and lack of social support is linked to an increased risk of heart disease, cancer as well as high blood pressure. There are a number of theories that attempt to explain the link, including:

- A good friend encourages their friends to lead healthier lifestyles.
- A Good friend encourages seeking help and access services, when needed.
- A Good friend enhances their friend's coping skill in dealing with illness and other health problems.

Good friends actually affect physiological pathways that are protective of health. Having close friends that you can count on, has far reaching benefits for your physical and mental health. A strong social network can be critical to helping you through the stress of tough times.

Dr. Edward T. Creagon is a cancer specialist at the Mayo Clinic, and said: "A prescription of friendship can go a long way toward a healthy future." There is mounting evidence from Sociologists, Psychologists and Medical Researchers who support, that strong social support like the term

'Connectedness' that is; to join together as by links or fastening; unite or combine, can help a person live longer."

Who is your friend? A faithful friend is a strong defense. Defence is described as, any thing that opposes attack, violence, danger or injury and anything that secures the person i.e. guards and protects e.g. a wall or barricade, safeguards. Just as God is the defence of the righteous, a faithful friend is a defence to his or her fellow friends. Solomon, who was the wisest man in the world quoted;

"Two are better than one; for the help each gets from the other. If one falls, the other can reach out and help. But someone who falls alone is in real trouble."

10

CHAPTER

FRIENDSHIP WITH THE WEALTHY

Wealth draws many friends to us; this is because when we acquire wealth it is then that we are able to provide the needs of others including; friends, family members and other colleagues. This in turn makes these friends and family members develop a special liking for us, as some of these people are pretenders, who love what is being done for them, and they are not the person doing the good. Many people prefer to befriend the rich, not because they love them, but because they will potentially gain materially from them.

"As long as you are prosperous, you shall have many friends: but which of them will regard you when you have lost your wealth?" (Anonymous)

This is simply the dark side of human nature and the reason why when one loses their wealth many of the people they regarded as friends and family flee without saying good bye. Your use has been served.

Therefore, we should take note, so when it goes well with us, we may not regard our many friends as all being genuine, because once we become poor the friendship may well be dissolved, not by us, but by the people we thought were friends.

FRIENDSHIP WITH THE KINGS CHAMBERLAIN:

"Then Herod went from Judea to Caesarea and stayed there a while. He had been quarreling with the people of Tyre and Sidon; they now joined together and sought an audience with him. Having secured the support of Blastus, a trusted personal servant of the king, they asked for peace because they depended on the king's country for the food supply." (Act 9: 20-21)

Blastus means sprout or shoot, meaning to develop or grow rapidly. He was a palace functionary or chamberlain, who had charge of Herod's bedchamber. He was probably a 'eunuch,' and had considerable influence over his master, Herod. This is the man, whom the men of Tyre and Sidon made friendship with. It is; therefore, wise to make friendship with people of great influence, people of high rank, the intellectual and wealthy.

FRIENDSHIP WITH THE KING:

"When Hiram king of Tyre heard that Solomon had been anointed king to succeed his father David, he sent his envoys to Solomon, because he had always been on friendly terms with David. In this way Hiram kept Solomon supplied with all the cedar and pine logs he wanted. And Solomon gave Hiram twenty thousand measure of wheat as food for his house-hold, in addition to twenty thousand

baths of pressed olive oil. And Solomon continued to do this for Hiram year after year." (1 Kings 5: 1-2; 10-11)

Hiram was a lover of David; he wished to maintain the same good understanding and friendship with his son Solomon. Hiram loved Solomon and supplied all his needs because of the friendship between them. It is good to keep up friendship and communication with families in a higher rank. It is of great wisdom to strengthen our friendship with those whom we find to be rich, but honest and fair.

YOU ARE KNOWN BY THE COMPANY YOU KEEP:
It has been said that a man is known by the company he keeps. By observing the friendly circle of a person, we can often tell his character and traits. If you move with drunkards you will accede to their habits. If you move with the intellectual, you will soon develop a way of thinking like them. And, if you move with the rich, the influential and the powerful, you will soon learn from them the art of becoming rich, influential and powerful. Rich, powerful and influential friends are the two sides of the same of the same coin. If a person has a lot of wealth he is also powerful. Also, a person who has political power and influence usually has a lot of wealth. In the company of such people or friends, you get more opportunities in life. People, who have the rich and powerful for friends can never remain poor. New opportunities always enter such a person's life.

FRIENDSHIP WITH THE POOR:

"If there is a poor man among your brothers in any of the towns of the land that the Lord your God is giving you, do not be hardhearted or tightfisted toward your

poor brother. Rather be openhanded and freely lend him whatever he needs. There will always be poor people in the land." (Deuteronomy 15: 7-8)

Therefore I command you to be openhanded toward your brothers and toward the poor and needy in your land." (Deuteronomy 15: 11)

A true friend should be ready to befriend, accept and give to his poor friends, not to avoid and harden his heart when they need help. God leaves the poor at the mercy of the rich to exercise the feeling of compassion and tenderness. The poor will never die away in the community, even the community that is blessed because poverty is not the penalty for evil. It is not always men's fault that they are poor, but the Lord makes some poor and makes others rich. To some he gave power to get wealth, from others he takes away power to keep the wealth they have. Are you poor? God made you poor, which is a good reason why you should be content and reconcile with your condition.

A GOOD REASON TO BEFRIEND THE POOR: Are you rich? God made you rich, which is a good reason why you should be thankful, and befriend and care for the poor. Let not the rich ignore the poor, for God can soon make them poor; let not the poor despond and despair, for God can in due time make them rich.

"He raises the poor from the dust and lifts the needy from the ash heap; he seats them with princes and has them throne of honour." (1 Samuel 2: 8)

The dump was the place where poor beggars slept at night and where they asked for alms during the day. But God is the human judge on duty, who gives favour to the poor. There have been many cases where, in the course of God's providence, a person has been raised from the lowest and most abject poverty state to the highest, from the plow to imperial dignity, from the dungeon to the throne and from the dunghill to nobility.

REPAY WITH USURY: Rich friends have forsaken the poor; they have not taken care of them, shown no kindness to them, nor made any provision for them. To reject the poor is a wicked act. Ahab took advantage of Naboth's property, which he had no right over. He took it not by secret fraud, by forgery, perjury, or some trick in the law, but avowedly, and by open violence. Those who make genuine friendships with the poor and care for them have not lost their gifts. No, what you give out or lend to others in obedience to the commands of God, is as done unto Him. One should regard his friends, especially the poor friends, who God has placed around you. He who looks down upon his poor friend sins against his Creator. Those that look down upon their poor friends because of their present conditions simply sin to the Almighty God. Those that look upon the poor with compassion, friendliness, care and love are here said to be in good condition, according to their character.

"He that has mercy on the poor is ready to do all the good offices he can to him, and thereby, puts an honor upon him, happy is he." **(Anonymous)**

He does that which is pleasing to God, which he himself will afterwards reflect upon the great satisfaction, for which the poor friend will bless him, and which will abundantly be repaid in days to come.

FRIENDSHIP WITH THE INFIRM AND DISABLED:

"The king asked, Is there no one still left of the house of Saul to whom I can show God's kindness?" Ziba answered the king, "There is still left a son of Jonathan; he is crippled in both feet (Disabled). When Mephibosheth, son of Jonathan, the son of Saul came to David, he bowed down to pay him honor, David said, don't be afraid, for I will surely show you kindness for the sake of your father Jonathan. I will restore to you all the land that belonged to your grandfather Saul and you will always eat at my table." (2 Samuel 9: 1-7)

When David was exalted to be king over all Israel, he sought to show compassion to the house of the fallen king and to repay the love, which his noble-minded friend, Jonathan once swore to him. Mephibosheth, the son of Jonathan was disabled in his feet. He was only five years old when his grandfather Saul and father Jonathan died. David sent for him and not only did he restore his father's properties to him, but took him to his royal table for the rest of his life. This was real favor and kindness. We should take pleasure in making friends with the disabled and the inferior. Though Mephibosheth was lame due to being disabled, unsightly and did not appear to have had any fitness for business, yet, for his father's sake, David took him as his own family. True friendship will be generous to all men at all times. Who is your friend?

TOUGH TIMES FOR THE DISABLED: *(See 2 Samuel 4: 4)* When the news of Saul and Jonathan came to Jezreel, the nurse of Mephibosheth was afraid that the enemy would send a party to Saul's house to kill the young master, who was next to the crown. She fled with the child in her arms to secure it in some secret place, and making more haste, she fell with the child, and by the fall some bones were broken, so that he was disabled or lame as he lived. See what sad accident human beings are liable to in life. Even children of princes and great men, the children of good men, are not always safe. What a reason we have to be thankful to God for preservation of our lives through many dangers. Just as God loves and protects us, so are we to love and care for the disabled.

GOD ALSO CREATED THE DISABLED? When a woman gives birth to a disabled child, her relatives often regard the event as a disgrace or a punishment metered out by God. Some even believe the devil had a hand in the matter or that evil spirits were at work. This explains why some families tend to hide their disabled children. Others refuse to admit their children are disabled and fear that no one will marry from their family. Knowledge, a sense of humanity, love and tact are needed to convince these families concerned to accept their disabled children and look after them. Indeed, there is a spiritual duty to accept them, care for and help them: Christianity unequivocally calls for sympathy for disabled people.

It is time we understood that the able and the disabled are all human beings created by God, therefore, disabilities of any kind can never be eliminated from the human race. Even a person with mental and physical disabilities, who lives in an institution, who has never spoken nor walked is still human. Psalm *139: 13* reiterates that God created our innermost being, that he knit us together in our mother's womb. What right do we have then to choose to abort a life that seems to be less than perfect?

UNDERSTANDING THE DISABLED: Disabled is when a person who has a physical or mental impairment that has affected their ability to carry out the normal day-to-day activities. Here are some examples of Physical **disabilities:** We are all familiar with seeing disabled people such as blind people with a white cane, guide dogs, hearing aids, crutches, wheelchairs, and prosthetic limbs and so on.

Mental Disabilities: These people have problems with thinking and reasoning, meaning they are unable to fend for themselves or operate in a normal day to day environment also unable hold down certain type of employment.

Disability from Birth: Many people are disabled from birth and this may be genetic or due to lack of oxygen during birth among other causes. Conditions such as Down's syndrome and spina bifida fall into this group as do those with cerebral palsy.

Disability Later in Life: This is often due to an accident that causes a range of circumstances, for example, brain damage, paralysis, or other injuries. Disease also has a role to play and conditions such as multiple sclerosis and Huntington's disease can eventually lead to disability. It is no wonder many of us feel unsure of how to relate to these people and are uncertain how our effort in communication will be received. Remember, they are disabled, yet human beings just as we are, just as we need love and friendship, the same way they need love and friendship. Who is your friend?

DARING TO BE A FRIEND TO THE DISABLED:

"I made the widow's heart sing. I was eyes to the blind and feet to the lame." (Job 29:13-17)

Job valued himself by caring for those that were disabled, that were supposedly not worthy of his favor. He counseled, advised and assisted them. We may come to be blind and lame ourselves, therefore should pity and care for those who find themselves in such conditions.

Disabled people are an integral part of our society; they have needs, desires and dreams, just like any other person. Their biggest problem is often the attitude of those around them. We tend to overlook, or completely ignore them. We often forget they are still human beings, except for the limitation of his handicap. The reason is often fear, and what do we say to them? Do they need assistance, how much do they understand?

The first step: Loving and making friendship with the disable is recognizing their humanity. This means treating them with respect and dignity. Job recognized the humanity of the lame and the blind and treated them with respect and dignity by inviting them to his palace and table.

The second step: Be of yourself, this is a good suggestion in relating to anybody, not just the handicapped.

The third step: Talk about the same things you would talk about with anyone else, like work, school, special interests, and hobbies and so on.

The fourth step: Help only when requested. If you feel uncomfortable with the situation, it is acceptable to make an initial offer to help, just as you might do with anyone when an able -bodied person falls, that person usually wants to get up on his own. When handicapped people fall, they may wish to get up by themselves. Similarly, many blind people prefer to get along without assistance.

The fifth step: Be patient. Allow the handicapped person to set the pace in walking and talking.

The sixth step: Don't be afraid to laugh with them: Anyone enjoys a good joke, as long as it does not make them the target of ridicule.

The Seventh step: Don't stop and stare when you see handicapped people you don't know. They deserve the same courtesy other able persons should receive. Staring at the disabled with your mouth open sends the non-verbal message that there is something wrong with them.

The Eighth step: Don't be over protective or helpful. The disable can do more than most people think they can, and they want to do more than most people will permit them. Let the disabled set the boundaries on what they are capable of doing.

Charity is essential for the disabled: The summary of the above mentioned action to help the disabled is called charity. Charity is another word for love not influenced

by selfish motives; it is the humane, sympathetic feeling, which seeks the good of others. It is that feeling that leads on the reformer, which inspires the philanthropist, which only blesses. It is the 'Good Samaritan' of the heart. It is that which thinks no evil, and is kind and hopes all things, believes all things, endues all things. It is the angel of mercy, which takes care of the unfortunate, which forgives seventy seven times, and is still rich in the treasure of pardon. It visits the handicapped, soothes the pillow of the dying, drops a tear with the mourners, buries the dead, and cares for the disabled and orphans. It is interested to do only good to those cast down by physical, mental disabilities, to deliver the suffering of the oppressed and distressed, to proclaim the Gospel to the poor. Whoever would be a true friend of the disable, and feel the real charm of goodness must cultivate this affection. Remember that genuine friendship to the disabled can mean the whole world to them. King David was a blessing to the disabled Mephibosheth because he possessed the spirit of kindness. Who is your friend? **(See**
Luke 10: 25-37 for the parable of the Good Samaritan)

11

CHAPTER

FRIENDSHIP AND GIFTS

"When the queen of Sheba heard about the fame of Solomon and his relation to the name of the Lord, she came to test him with hard questions. She arrived at Jerusalem with a very great caravan with camels, carrying spices, large quantities of gold, and precious stones." (2 Kings 10:1-2)

"Many curry favor with a ruler, and everyone is the friend of a man who gives gifts" (Proverbs 19: 6)

"On coming to the house, they saw the child with his mother Mary, and they bowed down and worshiped him. Then they opened their treasures and presented him with gifts of gold and of incense and of myrrh." (Matthew 2: 11)

It was customary in the east to show respect for persons of distinction by giving gifts of offering. When the fame of Solomon's great wisdom came to the ears of the queen of Sheba, she undertook a journey to Jerusalem to bring him gifts. She came with nothing mean or common; friends must devoutly give gifts to each other. What God favors you with you must honor him with it by giving to your friends. It is but a mock love which rests in the verbal expression of kindness and respect, while the wants of your friends call for real supplies, and it is in the power of your hand to bless them with gifts. It is no strange thing for our friends to desire basic necessities to help them survive in life. We must be ready, as we have the ability and opportunity, to give gifts to our friends. Who is your friend?

HISTORY OF GIFT GIVING: Since the dawn of time, people have given gifts. People in the earlier civilizations gave gifts to their tribal leaders and each other to show loyalty and love. Gift- giving has always been reciprocal, except for the heads of state in various cultures. They receive gifts in order to procure favour and to demonstrate allegiance, a practice still in place today. The Bible has many examples of gift -giving. The three wise men brought gifts to the holy child. Mary Magdalene washed Jesus' feet with precious oil as a gift. There are many worldwide gift traditions. In Egypt, idols and pyramids were built to honour the pharaohs, in the medieval age; gifts were given to kings to gain personal favor or allegiance in a war. Most of those gifts were silver, gold and other jewels. Gifts were also given to a beloved one or used as dowries for betrothals, which could include a herd of animals, or precious metals and jewelry. Today we give gifts for many reasons. Presents are given at cultural and religious occasions and seasons. We give gifts to mark birthdays, holidays, and farewells to show love, to say thank you or welcome.

LEARN THE ART OF GIFT GIVING: We give gifts or presents to family members, co- workers and neighbors. It is time to learn how to give gifts to our friends. The man or woman, who gets all they can and gives nothing, knows not real riches. It is not so much a question of how far we have gotten along in the world ourselves, as how many others we have helped to get on. Is there anything more unpleasant in this world than to have a lot of money but to help no friends? Friendship is no one-sided affair; it includes an exchange of gifts touching the soul. There can be no friendship without reciprocity. Many people view life selfishly rather than socially. They live to get, instead of to give and have found what all such persons find, namely, that the more one lives for self, the more material things satisfy. Giving a gift makes the giver feel good. Making your friends live richer rewards you with a feeling of achievement and caring, especially if the recipient shows gratitude and appreciation. Many a time, this is why we wish to be the gift giver rather than the recipient, but receiving is important in this reciprocal practice of gift giving.

Presents or gifts are exchanged by friends to show affection and respect to each other. They are the gestures that show how much you care. Buy gifts for your friends, to show your affection for them. Since the exchange of gifts has become a popular tradition of friendship, you would face no difficulty in finding the most appropriate gifts for your friends. You can give them jewelry, books clothing, accessories, etc. While presenting a gift to your friend, be sure to complement it with a nice bouquet of flowers, some candies, chocolates and a smile. It is definite that your gift would put a broad smile on your friend's face. Make sure that your friend becomes happy and feels special. Always remember in scripture it says that God loves cheerful giver. These are some of the things that create undying friendship and make the bond grow stronger. Who is your friend?

THE BLESSING OF GIFT GIVING (GENEROSITY):

In every heart, there are tendencies to selfishness, but the spirit of gift-giving counteracts them all. We cannot live in a world where all are so needy and dependent without gift giving. We do most for ourselves when we do most for others. In a moral sense, we know that 'it is more blessed to give than to receive.' Good deeds double in the doing. A large heart of charity is a noble thing, and most gift givers live nearest to God. They are planting the seed of charity that will grow to bless and save their posterity or household. 'He that will not permit his wealth to do any good to others while he is living, prevents it from doing any good to himself when he is gone.' Give and it shall be given unto you. One cannot receive all and give nothing, or give all and receive nothing, and to experience the joy and fullness of true companionship. There is power in the tender sympathy of a friend that can remove the darkness of hopelessness and cause to blossom the sunshine of hope and cheer.

FRIENDSHIP AND MONEY:

"Do not charge your brother interest, whether on money or food or anything else that may earn interest." (Deuteronomy 23:19)

"A feast is made for laughter, and wine makes life merry, but money answers for everything." (Ecclesiastes 10:19)

The special blessing of God guarantees riches and honor to all men, on the condition of their faithful adherence to his will. All things are at the call of money. By having money you can have what you wish. Money answers to every demand, hears every wish, grants whatever one longs for, and helps all. Meander said, *"Silver and gold - these are according to my opinion, the most useful gods; if these have a place in the house, wish what you wilt, all will be yours."*

Though wine make merry, it will not buy you a house, a bed, clothing, or become a supplier for the children, but money, if men have enough of it, will provide all of these things. Money, itself, answers nothing, it will neither feed nor cloth, but as the instrument of commerce it answers all occasions of this present life. What is to be had you may receive through money, but it destroys and separates friends when it is not properly handled.

"For gold the sovereign Queen of all below, friends, honor, birth, and beauty can bestow. The goddess of persuasion forms her train; and Venus decks the well-bemoaned Swain" (Francis Bacon. 1561-1626 English philosopher, statesman, scientist and author)

There is also the issue of the; first fruits principle through tithing, where God actually invites us to test him in our giving.

Bring the whole tithe into the storehouse, that there may be food in my house. Test me in this, "says the Lord Almighty, and see if I will not throw open the flood gates of heaven and pour out so much blessing that you will not have room enough for it." (Malachi 3:10)

FACTORS AFFECTED: William Shakespeare wrote: "Loaning money to a friend is a good way to lose both friend and money." Friendships are similar to a marriage, as they are built around the premise that through hard times a good friend will be there for you. In some uncertain economic times, some friends have no choice but to lean on other friends for financial help. Friendship may be affected by many factors. For example, a friend's perception of you may be lowered if, it is a repeated action. Even a good friend may feel you are not responsible with your life and are just taking advantage of them. You may notice that your friend sees you in a different way or starts to treat you differently. When that happens, it opens a door for quarrels and even violence, you may also feel inferior. All these factors may lead to the break-up of a friendship, if care is not taken.

One of the main reasons money can destroy friendship between, even the dearest friends, is the lack of communication. Making assumptions can lead to misconceptions about your friend and their financial situation, and unnecessary feelings of anger, envy or bitterness. We share our most intimate secrets with our friends. So why is it so difficult for us to mention monetary matters? Lending money complicates things by turning your friendship into a business relationship. If you feel comfortable doing it, and if you can afford it, go ahead, just don't expect to get the money back, even if it's a large amount. However, if you prefer to set it up a like loan, go through a third-party administrator.

"This is no time to lend money, especially upon bare friendship without security" (William Shakespeare 1564-1616 English poet and playwright)

Friends should feel free to give each other a treat now and then, but you don't want to be a doormat.

FAILURE TO PAY BACK:

"Let no debt remain outstanding, except the continuing debt to love one another." (Romans 1: 8).

This rule, together with other rules in God's word, would propose a remedy for all the evil of bad debt destroying friendships. Love is the only debt which can never be paid off, for it is always due. Do not continue in your debt, if you are able to pay it. Do not spend on yourself, which you owe to your friend.

"The wicked borrows and pays not again." (Psalm 37: 21)

When there is any kind of monetary relationship between friends, there is always a lie. Borrowing money and failing to pay it back opens the door to one lie after another, often with appropriate reasons: the first is to postpone the date of paying back, and the second is to keep the friendship alive. No matter what one intends to achieve, telling lies to one's friend, in the end the friendship stands the risk of being destroyed. Friendship is always threatened when there are unclear financial issues between two or more persons. Think of it this way: 'Give a man a fish and he eats for a day. Teach a man to fish, and he eats for life.' Offer to help your friend think of solutions to improve their financial situation so they don't have to rely on you so much. Also, don't be afraid to just simply say no when they ask for something you cannot afford. Doing favours is not the best way of winning friends. Just make sure to give your refusal a positive spin.

"To get rid of a friend, lend him money." **(Anonymous)**

FRIENDSHIP AND APPRECIATION:

"Boaz answered, 'I have heard about everything that you have done for your mother-in-law since your husband died. I know how you left your father and mother and your country and how you came to live among a people you had never known before. May the Lord reward you for what you have done? May you have a full reward from the Lord God of Israel, to whom you have come for protection?" (Ruth 2:12)

For those who do well deserve a commendation, those who leave all to help a friend are worthy of appreciation. Boaz recognized that he alone could not appreciate and repay Ruth for her care. He prayed that Ruth might be abundantly rewarded by the Lord.

Appreciation means to be grateful or thankful for anything.

"Nothing is more honorable than a grateful heart."
(Seneca 4BC-65AD Roman Stoic philosopher, statesman and dramatist)

I believe that everybody cherishes being appreciated. Most of us as little as children and young people had far too much criticism. So it is difficult to now give what we did not have and have not learned. Appreciation is like a smile, when you give it away, it comes back to you.

"Appreciation is a wonderful thing. It makes what is excellent in others belong to us as well." (Voltaire 1694-1778 French philosopher and writer)

Regrettably, it appears the virtue of appreciation has diminished in today's society. It now seems to be more acceptable, the 'in-thing,' to be rude, arrogant, outspoken and intruding, without any regard for the obvious effects. Human nature often drives us to find and point out faults and negativity to others. Yet we all have choices each day, we can choose to be positive and appreciative, or we can choose to be negative and snobbish.

Appreciation starts with little things, things we don't always notice or have come to be taken for granted. It is also directly linked to value, how much we treasure something or someone. Whether you are appreciating a family member, a friend, a co-worker, a customer or client, people need to be acknowledged for what they do, they need to know that they make a difference.

"Always remember, everyone is hungry for praise and starving for honest appreciation."
(David Berg 1919-1994 iconoclastic founder and spiritual leader)

HOW DO YOU SHOW YOUR APPRECIATION? We show appreciation in a number of ways, a simple smile and a thank you works well, but all too often we forget even to do this gesture. Another way we show appreciation is by shooting off a quick note of thanks in an e-mail. We can give a small, yet a personal, gift, to someone we appreciate. Another good way to tell your friend you appreciate their friendship and care is by writing it out. Send a text message that just says, "Thanks for being a great friend." Send them a 'thank you' card; take them out for lunch, and so on. Everyone loves feeling appreciated, so, no matter how you go about expressing your appreciation for a friendship, you probably can't go wrong. Just be sure you avoid any racial slurs, jokes, crude items etc, in your approach and you will be fine. Never forget, your friendships are all you take with you out of this life, so, make the most of them and be sure to show the people you love and appreciate how much they really do matter to you.

"Appreciation can make a day, even change a life. Your willingness to put it into words is all that is necessary."
(Margaret Cousins 1878-1954 Irish/Indian suffragette and Theosophist)

YOU ARE YOUR OWN BEST FRIEND:

"The second is this: "Love your neighbor as yourself is more important than all burnt offering and sacrifices."
(Mark 12: 31)

The Lord did not ask us to love our neighbors and forget about ourselves. To love God and our neighbor is the greatest commandment of all, yet we must not forget about ourselves. Our supreme and uttermost affection is to be reserved for God. But as sincerely as to ourselves, we are to love all mankind and with the readiness to love and befriend ourselves. We are to love and befriend ourselves by behaving with dignity and prudence, which might gain us respect. Give no person an occasion to look down upon you, and you will not be rejected, if you do not follow vanities and make yourself despicable and less important. Bearing in mind, if you cannot love yourself how can you love others?

CONTROL YOUR DESTINY: The only person, who has absolute control over your destiny, is no one else but yourself. You may have many friends and well-wishers like, your parents, siblings, neighbours, but the best friend you have is yourself. You must love, respect and esteem your very being. In short, you must be a friend of yourself. You must be a success with yourself, before you can be a success with others. It is advisable to listen to the words of your parents or friends, but the final decision must come from you. Learning to love and befriend yourself isn't easy, especially if you are a survivor of child abuse or neglect. Sometimes it can be hard to find things we like or love about ourselves. So, ask other people, a friend and a lover to tell you all things they like about you. The Lord Jesus asked His disciples what people said about Him. You may need to hear the things other people like about you before you can value them yourself.

When Jesus came to the region of Caesarea Philippi, he asked his disciples, "Who do people say the Son of Man is?" (Matthew 16: 13)

PRAISE SOMETHING IN YOURSELF:

"I am one of them that are peaceable and faithful in Israel." (2 Samuel 20: 19)

This woman could boldly speak something good about herself that she is for peace, and of no contention of any kind. She was faithful, and adhered to her prince and neither sought to rebel in the city. In this society, we are taught that praising ourselves is selfish and wrong. But praising ourselves for things that are good about ourselves only helps us. It is a healing thing to do, something that nourishes our self-worth. When we befriend and love ourselves, we are happier and more true to our own selves, and that happiness and ability to be free spreads to others. See yourself through gentle eyes, with compassion and love the way your friends do. Don't criticize yourself. Allow yourself to do comforting things for yourself. Let yourself feel how good you feel when you do those things, and tell yourself that you deserve to feel that way, to feel good. Above all, remember that you are a truly loveable person, and that you deserve only kind treatment, especially from yourself. God created us all in his own image, and he first loved us, so who are we not to love ourselves?

YOUR SPOUSE, YOUR FRIEND:

"His mouth is most sweet, yes, he is altogether lovely. This is my beloved, and this is my friend." (Song of Songs - Solomon 5:16)

Here is full assurance of hope among spouses. ***"This is my beloved, and this is my friend."***
See with what boldness they claim relation to themselves, and then with a triumph they proclaim it. 'It is property that sweetens excellence.' Not to see him or her as ours, would be a torture rather than happiness, but to make and accept our spouses as our lovers and friends is a complete satisfaction. Those who make their spouse as their beloved shall have them as their friends.

A SUCCESSFUL MARRIAGE: It is said that you should marry your best friend, and for a truly successful marriage, it will be between two friends. There are several sayings and studies that shows that you should be friends first, and lovers second. However, often times in marriage we get caught up in life and forget to do things to strengthen our friendship with our spouse. The result is that your spouse is no longer your best friend; rather your spouse becomes more like a roommate. Aren't best friends great? You laugh together, cry together, and just enjoy one another's company. Does this describe your relationship with your spouse? If not, it can. Friendship greatly contributes to the success of a marriage. It won't happen overnight, but the following tips will help you achieve a best friend connection with your partner.

View your spouse as your equal. Marriage is a partnership. What a relief to know that you don't have to micromanage your spouse or constantly tell them what to do. You would not remain friends with someone who bossed you around. So don't look down on them, instead, celebrate and cherish your spouse as a unique and equivalent mate. Do not compete with one another. Each individual brings unique contributions to the relationship. So, there is no need to compare yourself to your partner. Instead, travel the path together, enjoying each other's special qualities along the way. Where, one has a strength the other a weakness and vice versa, but together you are stronger.

Treat each other with kindness. Often commit random acts of kindness for your spouse. Fix their favorite meal without asking. Do not bully or manipulate to get your way. Your benevolent spirit may inspire your spouse to return the kindness back to you. Talk nice, try always to speak to your spouse in a loving tone. Never belittle or put your spouse down with words. Avoid talking to them when angry. Calm down first and then resume the conversation. This prevents speaking bad and hateful words that can't be erased later. Share everything. Adopt a what-is-mine-is-yours attitude. Enjoy possession equally, that includes your mind and emotions. Let them know the thoughts going through your head, meaning communicate all things, including the small irrelevant things. Tell them all about your dreams and desires. Sharing creates closeness. Spend time together. Physical separation spawns emotional detachment. So be in each other's presence as much as possible. When feasible, dwell in the same room when you are both at home instead of being apart. Make your friendship with your spouse a priority.

We need to ask ourselves if we're making friendship with our spouses a priority. Do we save our best energy for developing friendship with our spouses, or are we too busy? Sometimes you have to say no, to other pursuits so you can have time to protect and nurture the gift of friendship in marriage. The seeds of friendship we plant today will continue to bloom later in our marriages. We've all seen older couples sitting and eating the meals in complete silence. I want to grow old relishing my friendship with my wife. If you want the Lord to help you nurture your friendship with your spouse, this should be your prayer:

Lord Jesus, show me ways to nurture friendship with my spouse. So we can continue to enjoy each other through the passing years. Lord, today. I commit myself to making friendship with my spouse one of my top priorities. Where

I need to give up some activities so I will have time with my wife, give me eyes to see that. Thank you for the lifetime friendship you've given us in marriage. Amen.

WAYS TO RUIN YOUR FRIENDSHIP:

"A certain man in Maon, who had property there at Carmel, was very wealthy. He had a thousand goats and three thousand sheep, which he was shearing in Carmel. His name was Nabal and his wife's name was Abigail. She was an intelligent and beautiful woman, but her husband, was surly and mean in his dealings. Nabal answered and said "who is David? Who is the son of Jesse? Many servants are breaking way from their masters these days." (1 Samuel 25: 2-10)

Nabal was wealthy but poor in character. He ruined the friendship between David and his men and his family by his negative character. He was a friend who had no sense, either of honour or honesty; of honour, for he was mean and ill-humored; not honest, for he was evil in his doings, hard and oppressive, and a man that cared not about the impact of his negative character on his friendship. There are a lot of lonely people who claim to have real trouble establishing friendship. Usually, they are making simple mistakes that virtually guarantee the ruin of most of their chances. Here are some of the main ones:

1. Disrespectful behavior: Some people are so bad at giving respect, the only possible source I can imagine their attitude coming from is bad upbringing. They seem to see relationship as a kind of game, where they can only gain respect by stealing something from another person. They can't imagine that respect can be created out of thin air.

Showing respect for your acquaintance is the basic building block to establish friendship. If you are not willing to do so, don't be surprised if nobody likes you.

2. Constant complaining: Some people see friends as nothing but sounding boards for whining. All they talk about are their problems and how horrible they are. Such people need a big wake-up call. No human being cares about your trouble; only God does. Make your complaints to him through prayer and not your friend, so you don't ruin your friendship.

3. Revealing a precious secret: This is by far fastest of all. Once the secret is out, and an embarrassment ensues, there will be no doubt your friendship will go down the drain.

4. Making fun of your friend for no reason at all: If you know your friend is the serious type, then this could surely make them stay away from you for all eternity.

5. Deception: Once you deceive your friend, the trust that has been built over the years of the relationship, can be shattered right there and then.

MANY FAST WAYS: There are a many fast ways to lose a friend. Fast in the sense that the friendship could be over in just a nick of time. Friendship, just as well as any other relationship, is precious, it is so vulnerable and so delicate that once broken can never be put back. Though the pieces can be picked up, it can never be made up the way it was before. So if you are the type of person who values friendship greatly, don't ever try to do the above. Not only will it create you trouble, it will also ruin the most precious treasure you have got, 'your friend.' Remember, it is never easy to win friends, especially the friendship that can stand the test of time. Not everybody can find a friend who will stick with him or her through thick and thin.

HOW TO MAINTAIN A FRIENDSHIP:

"Be completely humble and gentle; be patient, bearing with one another in love. Make every effort to keep the unity of the Spirit through the bond of peace." (Ephesians 4: 2-3)

There is always the danger of discord, neglect and offense where friends are brought together in one society. There are so many different tastes and habits, and variety of intellect and feelings, the modes of education have been so various, that the temperament may be so different; there is a constant danger of division. Hence, there is so much need for caution and care. True friendship is called to unite together in the sentiment and affection of peace. Peace is a bond, as it unites people, and makes them live friendly with one another. A peaceful disposition and conduct binds friends together, whereas, discord and quarrelling disbands disunites their hearts and love.

POINTS TO REMEMBER: Focus on what you can give to a friend, not what you can get out of a friendship. Don't get caught up in keeping tabs on who has given most in the friendship. Give to your friends regardless of how little they give to you. Encourage your friend, real friends inspire and push each other to be the best they can. Rather than drag each other down, they are happy when other people achieve their goals. Be willing to forgive and don't let hurt turn to grudge. This is one sure way to destroy a friendship. Forgive your friend and move on. Tactfully point out their mistakes as this is one way to show your concern for others. If you really care, you will tactfully point out a specific example for their good. Don't harp on about problems all the time. Don't walk away from a friendship when you see some of your friend's faults, be patient with them as they try to adapt and change. Be reliable, so when you say you are going to be there, be there. Don't try to control your friend as real friendship does not mean you always have to be together. If you are afraid to let your friend(s) out of your sight, you are probably afraid of losing them. Good friends may learn to appreciate each other even more. Be there for good and bad times and celebrate with them, if your friend is excited about something. But don't be there only for the good times. Most of the time, what friends really need is a sympathetic ear, someone who understands their feelings. Learn to accept personality differences in friends. Be careful not to evaluate other people by how you react in a particular situation. Do not automatically take your friend's behavior personally. Don't be a blabbermouth so learn and be willing to keep each other's secrets.

CHAPTER 12

JESUS, FRIEND OF ALL

There is one Friend to whom the words of Solomon, "Your own friend do not forsake," are especially applicable. The best of our actions may become the worst of our accusations. It is true that the Lord Jesus Christ was a friend to sinners, the best friend they ever had, for He came into the world to save sinners. Having the Spirit of Christ living inside of us, we should not avoid sinners, but love them as our Lord did, for we were once like them. The Lord was accused of being a companion of sinners and seeking the society of the wicked. So will you be accused, as you make sinners your friends to bring them to God?

Friendship is the only cement that will hold the world together. Wouldn't life be miserable without friends? Everyone wants to think that they have at least one friend. Abraham Lincoln said, "the better part of one's life consists of his friendship." Why are friends so important? A friend is one who is your ally in trouble. He is one to who you can tell your troubles and deepest secrets, without fear of having them revealed. He is one who likes you because you are you, and not for what he can get from you.

"Your friend is the man who knows all about you, and still likes you." (Elbert Hubbard 1856-1915 American writer, publisher, philosopher and artist)

With this fact in mind, it is perfectly appropriate to think of Jesus as your best friend. He is a friend who is the chief and highest of all friends. There is no friend to whom we ought to be so intimately attached to rather than Him: 'Your own friend and your father's friend do not forsake.'

THE FRIEND OF SINNERS IS HIS NAME: Their friend thought of them with love when no other eye pitied them and no other heart seemed to care for them. *(See: Romans 8: 5-7)* Their friend entered with sympathy into the case of the lost, for 'the Son of man came to seek and save that which was lost.' Their friend gave them good and sound advice, for whosoever listens to the words of Christ shall find in His teaching the highest wisdom. Their friend laid down His life for the salvation of their souls, for is there no greater love than that a man should lay down his life for his friend. Jesus, friend of sinners, lived among them and ministered to them, Jesus took their sin upon himself to make reconciliation with God and prepare them for heaven. Jesus Christ had done for us all that had to be done. He had done much more than we can understand, so shouldn't this be our character towards our friends? A good friend would serve his friends in love and joy like Jesus did.

OUR FATHERS FRIEND: Abraham, Isaac and Jacob were our fathers. These men were friends of the almighty God. It is a very blessed thing to have the Lord Jesus Christ, who is God incarnate man, as having been our father's friend. Son of Joseph, Ephraim, had God with him. Happy that Joseph's father, Jacob, saw God at Bethel. Happy Jacob, whose father Isaac, walked in the fields and meditated in prayer with Jehovah. Happy that Isaac's father, Abraham, had spoken with God and was called 'the friend of God.' God has a habit of loving and blessing families. Our fathers' friend has made us kings unto God and princes in the earth in their absence. What a gracious loving friend our fathers had. Your own friend and your father's friend do not be forsaken.

OUR OWN FRIEND: The Lord Jesus Christ is our spiritual friend. Unseen, yet he is near and with us always. There is one we read of in the Bible who was David's captain of hosts and there was another who was David's counselor. But there was one man whom we always call David's friend, Jonathan, and I envy him such a title. Yet Jesus gives his name to all who put their trust in him and takes him as their friend. Now, if Christ is really your friend, you will have spoken to him, and placed your confidence in him. Also, you will have told Him about your lost estate and sinfulness, and have surrendered to him as your own Savior. You have committed your day-to-day activities to his hands, and left them there. If the Lord Jesus Christ is indeed your friend, then he has helped you. You were a stranger and he took you in, you were naked and he clothed you. You was spiritually sick and in prison and he came to you and healed you. He broke your chains and set you free taking your sicknesses and made you whole. He retrieved you from the grave, and went in your place, that by his death you might live. What a gracious friend! This is a friend you cannot live without. How loving and caring are we to our friends? Can our friends say all these things about us that are said about Christ Jesus? What a friend we have in Jesus.

Who's Your Friend?

HE IS ALWAYS OUR FRIEND: My own friend and my father's friend will never forsake me. It seems to hint that you may forsake Him, but it does not suggest that He will ever forsake you and He never will do so. If our gracious friend 'Jesus' had ever meant to do away with you, He had so many good reasons for doing so, that surely he would have done it earlier. But His love is constant to His friends. A friendship of true friend is constant, whatever a friend's shortcomings or faults are. So is the Lord Jesus Christ's friendship to all, He is a friend who loves at all times "while we were yet sinners Christ died for us." *(See Romans 5:8)* It is not the number of the so-called friends that helps us. What we prize is the one whose love is even stronger and purer than the ties of our siblings. Christ alone provides this super-excellent friendship.

For whoever does the will of my Father in heaven is my brother and sister and mother. (Matthew 12 vs. 50)

SIRACH'S WORDS ON FRIENDSHIP: *(Sirach circa 200-175 BC, wrote The Book Ecclesiasticus)* If you are polite and courageous, you will enjoy the friendship of many people. Exchange greetings with many, but take advice from only one person out of a thousand. When you make friends, don't be too quick to trust them, but make sure they have proved themselves. Some people will be your friend only when it is convenient for them, but they won't stand by you in trouble. Others, will fall out with you over some argument, and then embarrass you by letting everyone know about it. Some will sit at your table as long as things are going well, they will stick to you like your shadow and give orders to your servants, but they will not stand by you in trouble. If your situation takes a turn for the worse, they will turn against you, and you would not find them anywhere.

BE ON GUARD: Stay away from your enemies and be on guard against your friends. A loyal friend is like a shelter, find one, and you have found a treasure. Nothing else is as valuable, there is way to measure the value as you cannot buy it. A loyal friend is like medicine that keeps you in good health. Only those who fear the Lord can find such a friend. A person who fears the Lord can make real friendship, because he or she will treat their friends as they treat themselves. Never abandon old friends, you will never find a new one who can take their place. Friendship is like wine, it gets better as it grows older. Get to know the people around you as well as you can, and take advice only, from those who are qualified to give it. Engage in conversation with intelligent people.

GAIN HIS CONFIDENCE: If you stick something in your eye, tears will flow, and if you hurt a person deeply, you will discover their true feelings. If you throw stones at a bird, you will scare it away, and if you insult a friend, you will break up your friendship. Even if you have a violent argument with a friend, and you speak sharply, all is not lost. You can still make it up with them. But any friend will leave you, if you reveal hidden secrets, or if you turn on them unperturbedly. Gain the confidence of you friend even if he is poor, then you can share his happiness if he becomes successful. Stand by him when he is in trouble, if you want to share with him when better times come his way. Fumes and smoke appear before the flames do, insults come before violence. You should never be afraid to protect a friend, and should never turn a friend away when they are in need. If you suffer because of them, everyone who learns of it will be on guard against them. Anyone can claim to be your friend, but some people are friends in only name. The grief caused when a close friendship turns sour is as painful as death.

A real friend will help you against your enemies and protect you in a fight. Never forget such a companion in battle, share the results of your victory with those who are your Friends.